THE OUTDOOR CHUMS AFTER BIG GAME

Or

Perilous Adventures in the Wilderness

Captain Quincy Allen

The Outdoor Chums After Big Game

Captain Quincy Allen

PO Box 2211
Fairfield, IA 52556
www.1stworldlibrary.com
First Edition

LCCN: 2006935355

Softcover ISBN: 1-4218-2500-7
Hardcover ISBN: 1-4218-2400-0
eBook ISBN: 1-4218-2600-3

1st World Library Literary Society

Giving Back to the World

"If you want to work on the core problem, it's early school literacy."

- James Barksdale, former CEO of Netscape

"No skill is more crucial to the future of a child, or to a democratic and prosperous society, than literacy."

- Los Angeles Times

Literacy... means far more than learning how to read and write... The aim is to transmit... knowledge and promote social participation."

- UNESCO

"Literacy is not a luxury, it is a right and a responsibility. If our world is to meet the challenges of the twenty-first century we must harness the energy and creativity of all our citizens."

- President Bill Clinton

"Parents should be encouraged to read to their children, and teachers should be equipped with all available techniques for teaching literacy, so the varying needs and capacities of individual kids can be taken into account."

- Hugh Mackay

CONTENTS

CHAPTER I

GLORIOUS NEWS

"Hello, there, *Red Rover*! Come alongside!"

"What's the row, fellows? This dandy breeze is too good to be wasted loafing."

"Frank's coming in the *Jupiter*, and coming like a streak!"

"Yes, and more than that, Bluff, he waves his hat as though he had great news!"

Will Milton and Jerry Wallington sat in the double canoe, that with flapping sails pointed its stem into the wind; while their chum, Richard Masters, known among all his schoolmates as Bluff, manipulated the dainty fifteen-foot cedar craft in which he had been speeding over the surface of Camalot Lake.

Another midget boat, constructed on the same lines as that in which Bluff was seated, came flying down before the wind, and presently brought up alongside the other craft.

It contained a single young fellow, upon whose frank and open face rested a broad smile that seemed to prophesy pleasing news.

"What makes you look so happy, Frank? Evidently you've heard that your examination papers were up to the standard, and it's college next year for yours," remarked Bluff with eagerness, and, it must be confessed, a tinge of envy in his quivering voice.

"Right for you! But that is only the beginning of my news!" cried Frank Langdon as he reached out and caught Jerry by the arm.

"Am I in it?" demanded that worthy, seeming to catch his breath.

"Well, I should say you were, and with even better honors than poor me. Now, the rest of you fellows, don't look that way. It's all right, I tell you," went on the bearer of news, trying to control his own voice, but succeeding only a little better than Jerry.

"Say! do you mean it? Did Bluff and I get through, after all?" exclaimed Will.

Frank nodded his head enthusiastically.

"Careful, now, you wild Indians! Just remember that you're in canoes that can be upset easily, and unless you want a ducking out in the middle of the lake, restrain your enthusiasm a bit, please. It isn't the easiest thing in the world, climbing over the stern of a canoe with all your clothes on," he warned them.

"But is it really true?" pleaded Will. "Have I crawled through decently? Well, I'm glad; not only because it will keep four chums together a while longer, in college, but my mother has set her heart on this thing. Yes, I'm mighty well pleased."

Will's mother was a rich widow, and as he had only a twin sister, Violet, for whom Frank entertained a pronounced liking, the two were more than ordinarily dear to Mrs. Milton.

"Well, fellows, let's give one mighty cheer because of our good fortune," said Jerry, his face beaming with delight; for the chums were very fond of each other, and had a single one been left behind on the following year, when the college term opened, there would have been many a keen regret.

"Hip, hip, hurrah! Hurrah! hurrah! Tiger!"

No doubt, many persons ashore, who heard that lusty shout come ringing over the clear water of the beautiful little lake on which the town of Centerville was located, wondered what the burst of enthusiasm meant.

But then they knew these four boys were built along the right lines, and that while they loved the whole outdoors, with its attendant exciting times, never had they been known to indulge in mean pranks.

After the cheer had died away there was a shaking of hands all around.

"Fellows, it begins to look as though our great trip to the Gulf of Mexico last winter might not be our last grand outing, after all. You know what our parents promised us if we went through all right?"

"Hear! hear! Frank has the floor!" cried Jerry.

"We were to have our choice of an extended tour through Yellowstone Park to California, and return by way of the Canadian Rockies; or a grand hunt in the wilderness, wherever we chose to take it. That was the idea, wasn't it?" went on the happy occupant of the *Jupiter*.

"Talk to me about your personally conducted tours all you please, nothing appeals to me like a real old hunt in the Great West," said Jerry ecstatically. "Haven't I just longed for a chance to look at a big elk in his native wilds, for years? And the thought of a grizzly bear sends a thrill of pleasure through me."

"And as for me, haven't I lain awake nights without number thinking about what bliss it would be to actually snap off a few pictures of those same animals right where they live? How tame to go to a menagerie and get a photo of a poor old bear behind the bars, when a fellow has a chance to take him in the open!"

Of course it was Will who made this remark. He was the official photographer of the Rod, Gun and Camera Club, as our four boy friends called themselves, and his ambition to secure striking scenes, with wild game in the center of the stage, had already led him into quite a few scrapes, just as it would again when the opportunity presented itself.

"But what I have told you isn't quite all," remarked Frank presently, when the chatter of voices allowed him a chance to get in a few words edgewise.

"What else have you got up your sleeve?" demanded Bluff.

"Yes, confess everything, and perhaps we'll forgive you," came from Will.

"Well, I've had a letter." And Frank held something up.

"From that old side partner of Jesse Wilcox, the trapper whose camp we used to visit during our fall hunt?" cried Jerry.

Frank nodded his head.

"And what does he say? Hurry up, and tell. Can't you see that Bluff, here, will be overboard? He's leaning so far over the side that the water is ready to pour in over the gunwale. Will Martin Mabie take us out?" asked Jerry.

"He says he will be glad to do so, for old friendship's sake. I'm to wire when to expect us, and leave the rest to him," Frank explained.

"I hope he has told you what we are to fetch along. We've done some hunting, fellows, in our time, but that sort of thing, with big game in prospect, calls for heavier gear. None of your repeating shotguns need apply this trip, Bluff, you understand?"

Jerry could never become wholly reconciled to the modern gun Bluff owned. He professed to be such a clean sportsman that he always believed in giving the game a chance, and declared it to be next door to murder to have six shots in hand when hunting birds. With big game, it was all right, because then a fellow's life might often be in danger.

"Oh, Martin Mabie has written quite a long letter. He seems to be an educated man, and not at all the brand we figured out from hearing Jesse talk about him. Boys, we can now lay our plans, and make a start inside of a week," declared Frank.

"Isn't it just great? Did ever a set of grads get such a chance for fun as this?"

"I don't believe they ever did, or ever will, Bluff. And our folks have been mighty good to give us this glorious opportunity to enjoy an outing such as we've hankered after for a year, remember that, fellows," remarked Frank seriously.

"You can just wager that I make it a point to let the pater know my sentiments. He's the best dad going, and I mean to make him proud of me some day. But tell us more about it, Frank. Where is Martin Mabie to meet us, and what does he tell us to fetch along?"

"I'm not going to say another word, Jerry, until we get to the clubhouse, when every one of you can have a chance to read his letter," remarked Frank as he prepared to cast off and throw his sails to the breeze again.

"A week, did you say? Oh! what a long time to wait!" groaned Bluff.

"Still, there are lots of things to be done. I think it may be necessary for one of us to run down to the city to lay in some things in the way of ammunition, and a few articles of clothing for mountain wear."

"Then we'll appoint you as a committee of one to see to such traps, Frank," called Jerry as the other shot away with the wind, his canoe gliding over the little wavelets like a phantom craft.

Frank smiled. It was certainly nice to know that his chums felt such sincere confidence in him at all times. There was nothing he would not do to give them pleasure.

So the three cedar boats were soon heading for the clubhouse, and while they are thus employed it might be well for us to understand just who these chums were, and what they had been doing in the past to make them such firm friends.

Frank was from Maine, but his father, a banker, had come to Centerville a few years back; and among all the boys attending the Academy Frank had soon picked out as his especial friends these three, Will Milton, Jerry Wallingford and Bluff Masters.

After the Rod, Gun and Camera Club had been formed they had taken their first outing, using their motorcycles to reach the woods beyond the head of the lake. What befell them on this occasion has been told in the first volume of this series, called "The Outdoor Chums; or, The First Tour of the Rod, Gun and Camera Club."

Later on, a storm having done considerable damage at the school, they were given an unexpected fall vacation, and the chums decided to spend it on Wildcat Island, situated at the foot of the lake. There were several strange things connected with this island, such as a mysterious wild man who had been seen there; and besides, it was shunned because of the fierce bobcats that had possession. How our boys camped on this island, and what wonderful adventures they met with there, can be learned by reading the second volume, entitled "The Outdoor Chums on the Lake; or, Lively Adventures on Wildcat Island."

When the Easter holidays came around they had laid out another charming campaign. This was nothing more nor less than an expedition to Oak Ridge, that lay some ten miles back from the lake, amid the Sunset Mountains. Report had it that there was a real ghost to be seen there, and the boys were bent on discovering the truth of this weird story. It can be easily understood that they must have had a glorious time on that trip, viewed from the standpoint of an eager, adventure-loving boy. But the story is set down in full in the third volume, and you can read it for yourselves in "The Outdoor Chums in the Forest; or, Laying the Ghost of Oak Ridge."

No further long jaunts came the way of the quartet during the school term, up to the Christmas holidays, when they received permission to undertake a trip to the Sunny South. Just how this came about, and what wonders they saw and experienced on a Florida river, as well as upon the great Mexican Gulf, have been told in the fourth book of the series, called "The Outdoor Chums on the Gulf; or, Rescuing the Lost Balloonists."

And now it seemed as though, less than six months later, they were ready to embark on what promised to be the most exciting trip of all, a visit to the wilderness of the great Northwest, in search of big game.

Reaching the clubhouse, they quickly stowed their boats away. From this time on there would probably be scant time for aquatic sports. The tremendous undertaking they had in view would, very likely, occupy all their spare moments.

"Now let's have that letter, Frank. We want to con it so that every word will be photographed on our brains from this time on. Didn't old Jesse say that Martin Mabie was a big stockman now, and had really quit being a guide and hunter? Then it's mighty kind of him to undertake to convoy a raft of tenderfeet into the wilderness. Money didn't enter into it, that's sure," said Bluff.

"He mentions having had a long letter from Jesse," remarked Frank.

"That settles it, then. Our good old friend has been telling him everything we ever did, and got him interested. We must make it a point to run up and see Jesse before we go, and thank him."

"You're right about that, Jerry," said Frank warmly. "I was thinking the same, myself. But here's the letter. Read it for yourselves."

Various were the comments after this had been done.

"Talk to me about your good fellows! That Martin Mabie stands in a class of his own," observed Jerry. "Think of him offering to take us into the mountains for weeks, and see that we have the time of our lives! And he warns us not to mention the word money to him unless we want to break up the game. I sure am anxious to shake hands with that same friend of old Jesse."

"I move we start up there right now and see Jesse. The day is fine, and when can we spare the time better?" suggested Will, who secretly wanted just another chance to try a snapshot of the queer cabin which the trapper occupied.

"Second the motion!" cried Bluff eagerly.

"I'm some cramped, myself, from sitting so long in that canoe. Perhaps a run on our motorcycles might give me relief. So I say go," came from Jerry.

Frank himself believed it would be a good idea. He knew that once they started making preparations for their Western trip nothing was apt to tear them away.

"All right, boys. It's going to be a full moon to-night. Suppose we stop over and have a parting supper with Jesse? He'd be dreadfully tickled at the notion. Tell your folks at home, and meet me at the Forks in not more than half an hour."

Frank hustled the others out of the boathouse, locked the door, and then the four chums hastened to their various homes.

Ere the half hour was up they came together at the forks of the road, just out of Centerville. Frank was first on hand, as usual, but even laggard Will showed up on time, camera and all.

In single file, and with a little space separating them, they started off, the motors soon popping merrily as the boys entered into the spirit of the occasion.

The air was fresh as they sped along the dusty road. The leader was ever ready to signal a slow-down in case they met a farmer with a load of hay, going to market, or any other vehicle. This was rendered necessary because the cloud of dust might blind the eyes of those who came after, and a collision be the result.

In this fashion they arrived at the lumber camp, which was deserted at this time of year. From there on the pace had to be slowed down, for the road was only used by logging teams, and hardly suitable for motorcycles.

They were plugging along, each keeping his eyes open for obstacles apt to present themselves, such as roots cropping up above the surface, when the leader gave a sudden toot upon the little horn attached to his machine that warned the others a stop was imperative.

CHAPTER II

THE MOTORCYCLE THIEVES

"What's gone wrong, Frank?" demanded Bluff, dropping off his seat.

"In luck again, for I'd have banged up against that big root if Frank hadn't given the signal just then," chuckled Will, holding up his machine.

"A puncture, Frank?" demanded Jerry, who had been in the rear.

"Not at all. I thought I heard some one shouting. Perhaps I was mistaken, for with a lot of motors popping away it's hard to be sure. Still, we can stop for a minute and listen," remarked Frank seriously.

"Shouting - for help?" repeated Will, looking around nervously.

"That's queer," cried Bluff, "that we seldom go out anywhere but what somebody calls on us for assistance. Think of it! There was the town bully, Andy Lasher, who was caught under that falling tree in the storm, and rescued by Jerry."

"That's a fact; and then there was Jed, the bound boy, you remember, fellows," went on Will eagerly.

"Not to mention the saving of the aeronaut from the burning hotel by Frank, here; and last, but not least, our giving that little Joe the glad hand down South," observed Jerry, joining in with enthusiasm.

"Yes, but there are a few rescues you seem to forget, Jerry. How about that time when the wild dogs had you chasing around the tree?" asked Bluff, grinning.

"Oh, that isn't in the same class. You forget that I got out of that scrape by my own exertions," replied the other.

"But there was another time when we hauled you out of a hollow tree in which you found yourself caged. You didn't crawl out of there alone and unaided, if I remember right," persisted Will.

"Some things are better buried in oblivion. You and your camera want to remind a fellow constantly of events that ought to be forgotten. But Frank, that must have been an owl you heard. I haven't caught any call for help yet."

"Perhaps we'd better go on, then. Look out how you mount here, for it's a hard proposition, Jerry, with these roots and stones."

Frank had just started to move forward with his own motorcycle, when all of them heard a sound issuing from the woods alongside the "tote" road.

"Help! help!"

They looked at each other.

"Somebody's in trouble there. Who can it be?" said Frank as he leaned his machine up against a tree, as though eager to hasten to the assistance of the one who had cried out.

"No hunters around at this time of year," remarked Will as he followed suit.

"And the loggers have been gone some months," went on Bluff.

"Tell me about that, now! It wasn't a child's voice, or I might think a kid had got lost up here. Perhaps some man has cut himself badly with his ax," suggested Jerry.

"Or dropped down into some old abandoned mine shaft," spoke up Frank, with a wink toward Will; for one of the chums had gone through with just such an experience during one of their outings, and had to be rescued.

"Shall we all go?" demanded Bluff, given to caution.

"Why not? Nothing can happen to our machines here. For one, I decline to stay out of the rescuing party. Besides, perhaps I may get a chance to snap off a lovely picture of the Good Samaritans at work."

Will had hastily unfastened his camera, and held it in his hands as he spoke.

"All right, then. Come on, boys!"

With these words, Frank led the way into the woods.

"Sure the sound came from this direction?" asked Bluff.

"That was my impression. What do you say, Jerry?" and Frank turned to the chum on whose knowledge of woodcraft he felt he could rely.

"Straight in there. You're heading all right, Frank," he replied.

"How far did it seem to be?" went on the leader.

"That is hard to say. The man may have been weakened from

loss of blood. If he was shouting, then it may have been several hundred yards, perhaps a quarter of a mile off; but I think we'll come across him closer than that."

"I agree with you, Jerry," said Frank, stopping short.

"What did you hear?" demanded the other, for Frank had bent his head, and seemed to be listening over his shoulder.

"I don't know. Perhaps it was a bush springing back into place after our passage. But suppose we shout occasionally? It may encourage the poor fellow, and besides, guide us to where he lies," returned Frank, once more pushing on.

Accordingly they lifted up their voices and gave a series of calls.

"Why doesn't he answer us?" asked Will, astonished when only the echoes came back from the surrounding forest.

Frank stopped in his tracks.

"Can he have fainted from loss of blood?" said Bluff, still having in mind a picture of a woodsman who had severed an artery by a misblow of his ax.

"There's Frank listening again, and he seems to be paying more attention to our rear than ahead," remarked Will, puzzled.

"I bet you he thinks somebody is playing us for a lot of fools; that there isn't any one hurt, or in need of help at all. What's that?"

The distinct and well-known "popping" of a motor was heard.

"It's a trick, fellows! Somebody is meddling with our machines! Back to the road!" shouted Jerry, turning and plunging through the under-brush recklessly.

A wild scramble followed. The four chums were so excited, and filled with a determination to stop the unknown miscreants from making way with their machines, that they gave little heed to their steps. The consequence was that more than once a collision with a tree ensued, and various bumps afterward gave mute evidence as to the reckless manner of their chase.

"There's two of 'em!" shrieked Will from the rear, as he caught the sound of a second series of erratic poppings.

Evidently those who were meddling with the motorcycles did not have a thorough knowledge of how to work the same, for the sounds would suddenly cease and then start up again.

"Oh! don't I wish they'd just take headers over some nice fat root!" gasped the perspiring Will, still hugging his precious camera to his heart as he followed in Frank's wake.

The latter had made for the road in as direct a line as possible. Progress was bound to be slow through the dense undergrowth, and the sooner they struck the open the quicker they could hope to gain on the thieves.

In this fashion they came upon the road at last. Of course, their eyes immediately turned down its sinuous way to the quarter whence the excitable popping sounds still continued to come.

The sight that met their eyes amazed them. All of the chums had naturally expected that they would discover some mischievous school companions, who, seeing them coming, had hatched up this little game with the intention of playing a practical joke.

Nothing of the kind. On the contrary, they saw two of the motorcycles bobbing along in the most erratic manner possible, moving from one side of the rough road to the other, and mounted on the same were a couple of roughly dressed men, either tramps, or journeymen on the road looking for a job.

"Tell me about that, will you!" gasped Jerry.

"Why, the blooming idiots mean to steal our machines!" cried Bluff.

"Oh! what luck that I thought to take my camera with me!" came from Will.

Frank only made one remark, but it was characteristic of the boy:

"After them, fellows!"

Then began a mad chase. Had the road been half-way decent, the boys would have had no chance of overtaking the thieves; but those exposed roots, while not bothersome to the lumbermen, proved extremely so to the men who were trying to make off with the motorcycles.

They dared not put on great speed. More than this, much of their time was taken up with dodging the stones and other things that threatened to bring sudden disaster upon them.

Hence it was that the boys, having considerable sprinting ability, began to rapidly overhaul the fleeing rascals. The two men dared not cast a single glance behind, and consequently the only means they had of knowing how close their pursuers might be would lie in any shouts given by Frank and his chums.

As he ran, the leading boy cast an occasional look alongside the path. He was in search of a good stout cudgel. Knowing that the chances were the affair would presently come to a face-to-face issue between the two parties, he wished to be prepared as well as possible.

"Bully stunt!" exclaimed Jerry as he followed suit.

They were now drawing close upon the fugitives, who were having a nerve-racking time dodging those numerous roots.

Knowing that the angry owners of the wheels must be close upon them, the men endeavored to increase their speed, with disastrous results.

"Wow!" shouted Jerry, as he saw one of the riders suddenly shoot out of his saddle and take a header, to be followed by his companion a second later.

CHAPTER III

HOMEWARD BOUND, BY MOONLIGHT

"Jump 'em!" shouted Frank as he threw himself upon the first fellow, floundering in the road.

"I'm on!" echoed Jerry, suiting the action to the words by propelling himself straight at the second motorcycle thief.

This fellow happened to have come through his fall without getting hurt. The consequence was, he felt disposed to put up a much better fight than his confused companion, upon whose prostrate form Frank had straddled.

He rolled over once or twice with remarkable agility, causing Jerry to miss his guess when he thought to drop on him. Then, scrambling to his knees, the man, who turned out to be a rough-looking chap, indeed, pulled something out of his pocket, which he aimed at the two boys about to pounce upon him.

"Keep back, you!" he roared, his mouth being half filled with dirt after he had plowed up the earth of the roadway with his face.

"He's got a pistol!" shrieked Will, who was fingering his camera nervously from a point somewhat in the rear; and they immediately heard the little suggestive click that announced the pressure of a finger on the trigger.

Bluff was the quick-witted one on this occasion. He had his stick upraised at the time, ready to strike. Instead, he sent it from him suddenly with all his power, and as the cudgel was no light one, when it struck the extended arm of the kneeling thief the shock was so great that the shining object he had been gripping was hurled about five feet away.

Jerry instantly took occasion to possess himself of the same. The man was nursing his wounded arm and muttering to himself, his face screwed up with pain.

"Talk to me about your quick work! What could beat that, fellows?" cried Jerry as he stood over the grunting and disgusted rascal who had attempted to hold them off.

"What had we better do with 'em?" asked Bluff, frowning at the several scratches upon his machine caused by the accident.

"Any damage done?" asked Frank.

"Well, this man here has a sore arm, I guess; and the one you're sitting on looks as if his face might be a map, from the scratches," replied Jerry.

"Oh! I mean the machines," laughed Frank.

"Nothing serious here. How about yours, Will?" answered Bluff.

"Mine seems to be all right. They weren't going fast enough to cause a real wreck. A little paint will fix it up," was the answer Will made.

"Do you know either of these fellows?" went on Frank.

The boys took a better look at the men.

"Why, the one with the scratched face is Hank Brady, I'm sure. He used to live in Centerville. The other is a stranger to me," remarked Bluff.

"Well, I've seen him before. He was working in the office of the town paper as a tramp compositor a week ago. I suppose he got uneasy, and wanted to be on the move again, and seeing a fine chance for hooking a couple of motorcycles, they yielded to temptation. If we took them back they'd be locked up for this little job," observed Frank sternly.

"I hope you won't do anything of the kind, kids," said the fellow whose arm had been stung by Bluff's stick. "We only wanted to have a lark with you. Sure you don't think we'd be fools enough to run away with such valuable things as them motorcycles, when the telephone would get us at the next town? It was done for fun, but I reckon we paid the piper, all right," and he scowled at Bluff as he spoke, nursing his arm as though it were still painful.

Frank laughed. He was not of a vindictive nature. Besides, it did seem as though the two fellows had been punished enough already.

"No matter, it was a mean trick, and you deserve all you got. Get up, Hank. You took a lovely cropper that time. Where did you learn how to run a motorcycle?" he asked, helping the prisoner to his feet.

"I was a chauffeur a little time back. Sure we never thought to run off with the gas-wheels. Saw you comin' along, and Flimsy said it would be a good joke to make you fellers think somebody was sick in the woods. Then, when we seen you all go by, I said to him, 'Let's run a couple of them machines down the road a bit, just to tease the boys.' Flimsy he rode one once in his travels, and so we jumped on. The rest is history, and I got the map that goes along with it, on me face."

"What say, boys? Shall we let it pass?" asked Frank, winking at his chums.

Jerry, for reply, started to fire the revolver he held, until the entire six shots had been discharged.

"Here! Take your gun, mister, and next time don't be so quick to pull it on a stranger. Think what would happen to you if you'd fired and hit one of us? Some time you may even be glad that Bluff, here, was so quick with his stick."

He handed the empty weapon over to the tramp printer, who let his head fall, as though really ashamed of his action.

The boys started back to where the other machines had been left, while the two men slunk into the shelter of the woods, to patch up their hurts as best they might.

"Say! that was a queer ending to a rescue, wasn't it?" asked Bluff.

"I only hope my picture comes out all right. It ought to show Frank sitting on top of Hank, while Bluff and Jerry surround the other tramp, who is on his knees, aiming his old gun. Then my machine is lying there. Fellows, what need of words to explain what happened?" chuckled the gratified Will.

Whenever he succeeded in securing a coveted picture the ardent photographer was the happiest boy in the county. His pleasure caused him to fairly bubble over with good nature.

"Tell me about that, will you!" said Jerry, pretending to scorn such anexhibition of joy over so trivial a matter. "Why, you'd think the chap had knocked over some big game, to hear him chatter."

"And so he had," declared Frank quickly, "according to his light. All of us are not made alike, Jerry. One man's food is poison to another. You and I are fond of fishing and shooting, but Will is more of an artist. He delights in stalking the timid deer in the close season, and shooting him with his camera. Lots of people believe his way of securing pleasure beats ours all hollow."

"Anyhow, it doesn't thin out the game," asserted Will stoutly.

Jerry stopped short to turn a look of pity on his comrade.

"Think how hungry we'd all go out in camp if we depended on your blessed old box for supper," he suggested witheringly.

"All very true," remarked Frank as they reached the other motorcycles, and prepared to continue their interrupted journey to the camp of the trapper; "which is proof of what I say, that many men, many minds. There's room for all kinds in a party."

"Yes; and nobody likes to look over my prints more than Jerry," grumbled Will, feeling quite offended.

"Don't pay any attention to him. He doesn't mean anything by it. You know how he likes to joke every one. Now, we're off again, boys."

Once more they made their way along the rough road. The sight of those two unfortunates sprawling upon the ground was a lesson, warning the riders against trying for speed under such conditions, so they made haste slowly.

Upon arriving at the cabin home of the trapper they surprised him very much; and when Jesse Wilcox learned the object of their visit he was more pleased than ever.

They spent some hours with him, and even assisted in getting the evening meal. From their long experience now the boys had become quite proficient in this line, and were able to show old Jesse quite a few tricks that delighted him.

With the campfire blazing merrily, they ate supper alongside his rough cabin home. Of course, they fairly deluged him with questions about the habits of the big game of the West, which he answered to the best of his ability.

"Wait till we get out with Martin Mabie, fellows. He's on the ground, and can set us straight. Jesse has been trapping these little animals around here so long now he's a back number," joked Jerry, at which the trapper laughed, for he was very fond of these four lads, and nothing they said annoyed him.

As they had planned, the run home was made by moonlight. This necessitated that they walk with their machines until the good road was gained, below the lumber camp.

"I wonder whether those two tramps hit the high places, and got out of this neighborhood for keeps?" Bluff was saying, after they had mounted and were bowling along merrily toward town.

"The chances are that way. That tramp printer must be a bad sort of chap, it seems to me, and if Hank keeps along in his society I can see his finish," answered Jerry over his shoulder.

They had not made more than a mile when once more Frank gave a quick toot of his horn that brought the little procession up in a hurry.

"What ails us now?" demanded Bluff.

"Frank's bending over something in the road, as sure as you live!" called Will.

"Tell me about that, will you! Seems as if our lively times haven't stopped yet. It never rains but it pours, fellows. Hi! Frank, what's the matter? Say! Would you believe it? There's a man lying in the road!"

Jerry made haste to push his heavy motorcycle forward so as to reach the side of his kneeling chum.

"It's Hank Brady, boys, and he seems to be in a bad way.

Something has happened to him since we saw him last," said Frank, looking up.

"Goodness gracious! Is he dead?" gasped Will, his eyes dilating in horror.

"I don't know yet, but I'm going to find out," replied Frank, bending over so that he could press his ear upon the breast of the man in the road.

"And that tramp printer, where's he at?" asked Jerry suggestively. "Tell me that, will you?"

CHAPTER IV

STARTING HANK RIGHT

"He's alive, all right!" was the announcement of Frank presently.

"I hear water close by. Hold on, and I'll get some," said Will hurrying away.

Even Jerry was desirous of helping as best he could. He took hold with Frank, and the insensible Hank was carried alongside the road, to where some grass grew, and offered a softer resting place.

Had it been a friend who was thus in need of succor, they could hardly have shown more energy in attending to his wants.

"He's coming to," said Bluff after Frank had sprinkled the scratched face with some of the cold water.

There was a deep sigh, then Frank saw that the fellow's eyes had opened, and were surveying him with a troubled stare.

"Feeling better, Hank?" he asked quietly.

"Oh, I'm all right, I reckon. What brought you fellows here? Where am I, anyhow? Did I just drop off that motorcycle? No. I remember, now. Flimsy took the last cent I had while I lay in the road. The meanest skunk I ever met up with. If ever he crosses my path again I'll get even with the cur," he growled, sitting up and holding a hand to his head.

"What happened to you, Hank? Why were you lying in the road? Did you have a fight with that tramp printer?" asked Frank, suspecting the truth.

"Yes. I told him I was sick of keeping with him. He's a bad one, and some fine day he'll land in the stone jug. He scared me the way he talked. I started to tramp back home, and he kept nagging me all the way here. In the end he made me so mad I just tackled him. That was what he wanted. Why, he put me to sleep the easiest way you ever saw. I just remember him fumbling in my pockets before he hoofed it."

"Well, it was a lucky thing for you, Hank, after all. If you'd kept with that rascal you'd soon have been just like him. Did you say you meant to go back home now?"

"That's what I meant to do, but he's fixed it so I can't," muttered the other, grinding his teeth in fury.

"How's that?" pursued Frank, believing there must be a story back of his words.

"He took the ten dollars I stole from my dad. I won't never dare face him and say I lost it. I thought I could put it back in the bureau drawer, and he'd never know. I'll have to foller that Flimsy, and make him give it back."

"You can't do that for he'd only laugh at you, and perhaps beat you again."

"The thief ought to be arrested," grumbled Bluff indignantly.

"That would blow the whole thing, you see, and dad he'd know I grabbed it. I'm gettin' all I ought to have, I reckon. P'raps I might earn that ten some way, and hand it over. If I could only get another job as chauffeur it'd be all right," Hank Brady was mumbling to himself dejectedly.

"Perhaps you can," said Frank quickly. "I remember, now, that our man had to go away suddenly the day before yesterday. Look here, Hank! Do you really mean to do the right thing now? Have you had your lesson pounded into you?"

"I sure have. Never again for me, I give you my word. I guess my folks has been worried some on my account, but they don't need to any more. I've reformed, I have. I'm goin' to walk a straight line after this."

The fellow spoke as though he meant it, and Frank believed he could detect the ring of sincerity in his voice.

"All right. Shake hands on that, Hank. Don't you forget it, that you'll find plenty of fellows willing to give you a lift, just as quickly as some others want to give you a drag down. It all depends on where the other chap is standing himself. You come and see me to-morrow, some time. I'm Frank Langdon, and my father is the president of the First National Bank."

"This is mighty white of you, fellers," muttered the other, apparently ashamed.

"You can never pay it back to us, Hank, but some time pass it along; hold out a helping hand to some other poor chap in trouble. I guess if you know how to run a car decently you will get the job, if I speak to my dad. Now, another thing - that ten dollars you wanted to put back, was it in one bill?"

"Two fives," replied Hank, catching his breath.

"Then perhaps we can fix it up. I've got one here. Jerry, can you help me out?" asked Frank, who believed in doing the whole thing, once he started.

"Just happen to have it, by good luck," replied the other cheerfully.

"Say! that's too much, fellers - an' after I played that mean trick, too!"

"Don't worry about that. I'm not giving you this, Hank, only loaning it to you. You can pay it back out of your first month's salary. Here you are, and don't think for a minute that you're getting the best of all this. We're enjoying it, in our own way, more than you ever can. See you to-morrow, then. Good-night, Hank!"

They left the fellow standing there, quite dumb. He had tried to answer them as they rode off, but not a sound could he utter.

"Talk to me about the queer things that crop up with us, will you!" laughed Jerry as he kept close at Frank's heels. "Did you ever really hear the equal of that, now?"

"Oh, it's an old story. The only decent thing about it is the fact that of his own free will Hank was breaking away from his evil associations and heading back home, when he met with this last trouble. I say, Bluff!"

"Hello, Frank! What is it?" came from the rear, where the party addressed was following in the wake of his chums.

"How about Hank? Do you know if he ever played chauffeur half-way decent? I'd hate to risk the pater's neck with a greenhorn."

"Come to think of it, he used to run old Cragin's car for quite some time. Had an accident, and was discharged; but some people said Hank wasn't to blame; that it came about because the old man was too stingy to buy the right kind of tires, and always picked up job lots."

"Glad to hear it. He won't have that fault to find with the governor. Well, here we separate, fellows. To-morrow morning, at the boathouse, about eight, to lay our plans and arrange for the trip to the city."

With a cheery good-night the chums separated, and each headed for his home.

In the morning they once more came together, and for some hours there was an earnest talk, during which many ideas were put forward, and order gradually took the place of chaos.

A knock at the door took Frank thither, for he suspected who the visitor might prove to be, as he had left word at home to send Hank Brady there, if he called. Hank was now decently dressed, and his face did not look so very bad, though it bore a number of scratches.

"All right, Hank. I'm going with you to the bank. My father knows all about it, for I thought it best to start square, so that you need not fear about his finding out anything about your past," he said, shaking hands with the other.

"And he don't give me the shake on that account?" asked Hank eagerly.

"Of course he doesn't. He even said that what we did was right, and that he could look back to a day in his boyhood when a kind word started him along the straight and narrow path. My dad's the right sort, Hank. Serve him decently, and you'll never want a better friend. But at the same time he hates deceit, and will not put up with a sneak. You've got the chance of your life to make good."

"And I'm going to make good, all right, or bust tryin'. I'll never get over the white way you fellers acted with me, never, if I live a hundred years!" said Hank in a broken voice.

Frank took him over to the bank, where Mr. Langdon was

favorably impressed with his looks, and engaged him, after he had learned what he knew about the running of a car. Hank had worked in a garage for a year, and this knowledge was invaluable to him in his business as a chauffeur.

That afternoon Frank and Bluff started for the city, with a list of things they believed should be purchased before they went forth upon their journey. Bluff had in mind a wonderful hunting-knife, with an ivory handle, a picture of which he had seen in the catalogue of a sporting goods house, and he was secretly determined to possess such a magnificent tool.

"The time might come when a fellow would have only his trusty blade between himself and death, and then you just bet he wants a good one. Think of a big grizzly trying to hug you! Where would your little knife be, then? You'd soon wish you had that Cuban machete that hangs on the wall of your father's den, Frank," he said, when the other expostulated with him about purchasing such a murderous-looking weapon.

And Bluff did buy it, too. All the way home he kept tabs on that package, and often, when Frank was not looking, he would go through certain gestures with it gripped in his hand, as though practicing against that day when the aforesaid grizzly and he would have their little heated argument for supremacy.

Jerry, too, either felt shocked at the enormous size of the wonderful hunting-knife, or else pretended to be. He shrugged his shoulders in that scornful way he had, and turned his back on the prize Bluff had drawn.

"What else could you expect of a man who goes after quail with a Gatling gun? Why, the poor innocent grizzly will faint dead away at sight of that cavalry sword. It gives me a cold chill just to look at it," he observed.

Bluff only laughed.

"Rank envy eating up your soul, that's all, my boy. Wait till you see me in action with that razor-edged tool. I'll have you all turning green with envy yet," he said, fondling the ivory-handled weapon ere he thrust it back into its sheath.

The days dragged along. Will counted them, and each night heaved a sigh of relief that they were a notch nearer the time of departure. Finally the last night arrived, and their coming tour was to be marked by a little gathering at the home of Frank, which was intended to be in the way of a send-off.

CHAPTER V

WESTWARD BOUND

There were just eight people gathered together that evening to have a good time. Besides Nellie Langdon, of course, Will's twin sister, Violet, graced the occasion with her presence; then there came Mame Crosby, the vivacious girl with the auburn locks, who was so fond of teasing Jerry; and last, but not least, pretty Susie Prescott, a dainty, prim little blonde, whom Will considered a bundle of sweetness.

What a splendid time this congenial little company had! For many a day the memory of it would follow the four chums while far away.

All of the "material of war," as Mame called it, had been brought to Frank's house, so that it might be packed in one big trunk. Thus the boys would be bothered with only a suitcase and a gun apiece in the long journey across the continent.

The girls insisted upon being shown the wonderful aggregation of clothing and weapons. It was to them very much like a shopping expedition, and many were the exclamations of awe and curiosity as they looked upon the exhibition.

Bluff, of course, was very proud of that wonderful hunting-knife of his. He even smiled to see the perceptible shudder with which Nellie surveyed him as he cut imaginary circles in the air with the keen-edged weapon.

"Oh! I hope you won't have to use it very often, Bluff! It makes me shiver just to think of you meeting one of those fierce grizzl y bears,such as I have seen in the menagerie," she said confidentially to him.

"But you wouldn't have me leave this jewel at home, would you, Nellie?" he asked in dismay.

"Oh, no! Not for the world! - since you say that perhaps your very life may depend on having it; but please, Bluff, be very careful. You might cut yourself by accident, you know, and then - well, your mother and father would grieve so much if anything happened to you."

"Well, would you care?" asked Bluff boldly.

Nellie gave him an arch look and ran down-stairs, as she said that she was needed just then to superintend the placing of the refreshments on the table. Bluff laid the wonderful hunting-knife, sheath and all, back on the stand where his things were gathered, and smiled as if pleased. He had occasion, later on, to recall each little incident of that evening, when worrying his mind over a most mysterious thing that puzzled him.

The little company separated about eleven, for the boys expected to leave home long ere noon on the following day, and had a strenuous journey before them.

After an early breakfast they gathered at Frank's, where the last packing was done in hot haste, as the time was short. So it happened that none of them had more than a confused idea of what was done during that last hour, save that, some way or other, their things were crammed into the big trunk.

"We should have taken two, hang it!" grunted Bluff as he tugged at the metal catches, while a couple of his mates sat on top to induce the lid to come down.

"There! It's all right now!" cried Will, as the click of the catch announced the desired union.

So the trunk was snatched up by the waiting men and carried off, to be taken to the station. Frank and his chums quickly followed. Quite a gathering of relatives and friends were on hand to see them off.

Frank was taking a last look into the automobile, to make sure nothing had been forgotten, when Hank Brady, who seemed to be making good with his job, plucked at his sleeve.

"Hello! Came near forgetting to say good-by to you, Hank! Hope you get on fine and dandy while I'm gone," said the boy, holding out his hand.

"Thank you, Mr. Frank; but I only wanted to say a few words to you about a brother of mine who is out there somewhere, we believe. Now, I know the Northwest is a big place, and you might as well think of lookin' for a needle in a haystack as for a certain feller there; but accidents do happen, and by some sorter luck you might just happen to run across Teddy," said Hank quickly, and with a wistful look on his face that held Frank's attention.

"And if I do, what then?" he asked softly.

"Tell him his mother's still a-grievin' after him. You see, he is her baby, though a big feller for his age, which is seventeen about. He left us in a huff two years back. We heard in an indirect way several times, but never straight. She worries when she thinks nobody is a-lookin'. If Teddy would only write to her I think she'd be kinder reconciled," went on Hank, heaving a deep sigh.

"All right. If by any good luck I happen to run across your brother, you can depend on it I'll do my best to make him write. But how am I to know him among the thousands of people I meet?" remarked Frank as he was about to turn away.

"Well, he has -"

Just then some one pounced on Frank, and dragged him off, so that he never really knew how he was to recognize this wandering brother of Hank Brady in case he should meet him.

The train was almost due, and general good-bys were quickly said. Such a chattering as ensued, which kept up until the four chums climbed into the car that was to take them to the nearest city, where they would board the through train for the Northwest.

After the last glimpse of their loved ones had been lost by a sudden bend in the road, they settled down to making themselves comfortable. It was expected that they would make connection in St. Paul with the western through train bound for Seattle. Then would begin the grandest ride on the whole American continent, over boundless plains, and finally up into the majestic mountains.

Day and night they would be carried swiftly onward across the many miles of entrancing scenery. Wonderful sights would fall to their portion.

St. Paul was reached in due season, and once more they started forth, this time headed west, with the hunting-land beckoning them on.

"Tell me about this, will you!" remarked Jerry, after they had crossed the broad prairies and were climbing the tremendous heights that lie like a barrier between the center of the continent and the Pacific Slope. "How much more of it do we have before us, Frank? I'm getting so filled with wonder and awe that my tongue is getting into a rut with saying 'Ah!' so much."

"Less than a day will see us through now. Once we get over this range there lies a long valley, and in that is where Martin Mabie has his ranch."

"Then we'll do our hunting along the sides of the mountains?" suggested Will, who had used up nearly half his supply of films already, taking views of the wonderful things they saw on the trip.

"That's my impression, from what he wrote," replied Frank.

"And he also said game was fairly plentiful, if I remember aright," remarked Jerry.

"Well, he did say that they had been so busy of late on the ranch that no one had had time for hunting, and consequently the game had not been bothered very much; which, I suppose, amounts to the same thing."

"H'm! I hope he won't be so rushed with work that he can't take the time to go with us. Half of the fun would be lost if Mr. Mabie couldn't be along; for Jesse says he is the most entertaining man alive," grunted Bluff.

"Oh, you forget that he said by the time we got there the work would slacken up, and he promised himself a vacation, just to renew his old pleasure of camping out in the wilderness, away from all mankind," laughed Frank.

"That relieves my mind some," declared Bluff, brightening up.

"You're getting tired of all this travel, that's what ails you," said Jerry.

"No; it isn't that," remarked Frank. "Bluff has confessed to me that for the life of him he can't remember putting that beautiful hunting-knife in the trunk along with his other traps; and if he left *that* behind, half his pleasure would be lost. Now you know what's the matter."

"Not that I wish it to be so, but if such should prove to be the case, there'll be one delighted grizzly bear out in these same mountains - the chap Bluff calculated on carving with that big sticker," remarked Jerry jocosely.

But Bluff would not even smile. Truth to tell, he was counting the hours until he could open that trunk and relieve his distressed mind.

"Did you ever see a wilder bit of country?" said Frank, peering out into the gathering dusk, and trying to imagine those wooded hillsides populated with elk and buffaloes, and all the big game of the past, when a white man was never known west of the Great Lakes.

"Well, to tell the truth, I was thinking of that account I read in the paper we bought, about the work of a sheriff's posse in this region, chasing the bad men who held up a railroad train not a hundred miles away from here. It wouldn't be a pleasant experience for us to meet with, eh, fellows?" asked Will, who was known to have a timid streak in his make-up.

"Talk to me about your croakers!" jeered Jerry. "Will, here, is enough to freeze the marrow in one's bones. There isn't one chance in a thousand that such an adventure will come our way, and he knows it."

"Goodness! What a jar! The engineer must have thrown the air brakes on then in a big hurry! We're coming to a sudden stop, too! Oh! I wonder if anything can have happened? Are we going to have an accident, fellows?" cried Will.

With much creaking of the wheels the heavy train came to a stop, and at the same moment the four chums, listening with considerable apprehension, caught the sound of many loud and excited voices just outside the car.

CHAPTER VI

AT THE VALLEY RANCH

"Listen!" exclaimed Frank, holding up his hand.

"Talk to me about your Tower of Babel! It wasn't in the same class as that row. Twenty men trying to talk all at once!" growled Jerry, starting up.

"Oh! Where are you going?" asked Will.

"Outside, to find out what the trouble is," replied the other.

"But you may get hurt if those bad men start to shooting up the train," expostulated the official photographer anxiously.

Jerry gave a hoarse laugh.

"Tell me about that, will you! He actually believes we are going to be put through a course of 'stand and deliver' by the merry gentlemen of the road. Why, bless you, my boy, didn't you hear one man say something about a trestle burning just ahead? It spells delay for us, but that's the worst of the whole affair."

"Then I'm going out, too," declared Will, with sudden zeal, as he snatched up his camera and threw the strap over his shoulder.

He scented a chance for a striking picture, and to obtain that Will would have risked even a possible encounter with train robbers.

Frank and Bluff would not be left behind, and quickly the entire quartet had reached the platform. They found that the stop was at a little country station. A signal had suddenly flashed before the eyes of the engineer, telling him he must not think of running past, which accounted for the quick work of the compressed-air brakes.

No need to tell what was wrong. Up the track a quarter of a mile could be seen a fire, and one glance was enough to tell the chums that, just as Jerry had said, a trestle of some sort seemed to be burning.

Loud shouts attested to the fact that every available man was hurrying to the scene, in the hope of saving the trestle before it was so far gone that nothing could be done.

"Come on, fellows! Our train must stay where it is until this thing is done burning, one way or the other. Perhaps we can help put the fire out with buckets."

That was the first thought Frank had, to be of some assistance.

The four of them ran with the rest of the passengers. Such a spectacle could not be witnessed every day, and every one was desirous of getting closer to the scene of action.

"How did it catch?" asked Frank of a railroad man who was hustling about, handing buckets to a line of men extending down to the water of the creek far below.

"Don't know. Perhaps from sparks left by the six-seventeen freight. Lend a hand here, lads; we need all the help we can get," replied the other.

"Sure! That's what we came for. Get along, boys, and pass

these buckets!" cried Jerry, suiting the action to the words.

Once the string of buckets got to going, and the contents began to be cast upon the creeping flames, there sprang up a hope that the trestle might be saved.

Seeing this, the workers redoubled their efforts, and faster rose the full buckets, the empties going down at the same rate. It is really astonishing what a large amount of water can be carried by such an endless chain.

"Hurrah! We're besting it, lads! Keep it up!" shouted the agent, who was the man Frank had first addressed.

Will had not joined the relay. There seemed to be plenty of recruits without him, and, truth to tell, he was bent on getting a picture of the scene. Doubtless many present were startled by a sudden brilliant illumination as he set off his flashlight cartridge; but those who were in ignorance as to what it meant were soon set wise by others.

Once they began to get the upper hand of the fire it became easy. Fortunately, there was not a breath of wind at the time. Had it been otherwise, no efforts on their part could have saved the trestle.

"I should think they would have them all of steel!" gasped Bluff, as he labored away, passing endless buckets up and down.

"Most of them are, I understand, but in this case, you see, it is a long stretch, and perhaps it wasn't thought necessary," replied Frank.

"We're going to save it, all right; but I wonder if our train dare pass over? It seems to me the fire must have weakened the structure more or less," remarked Jerry.

"Oh, well, they'll find some means of strengthening it in that case. I'm only worrying about the delay. Mr. Mabie will have to wait so long."

"But, Frank, they must wire the news, and he will know the reason for our hold-up," said Will quickly, and the others all agreed that this must be so.

Less than an hour later the last spark had been extinguished. Then men climbed all over the trestle to ascertain just how much it had been weakened by the fire.

There was a difference of opinion among them, some declaring that it was as good as ever, and the others shaking their heads solemnly, as they prophesied all manner of dire things if the through train, with its heavy sleepers, attempted to go over.

While some gangs of men were hastily bracing up a weak spot with what material lay close at hand, kept for an emergency of this sort, a freight train that happened to be on a siding at the station, was pushed out on the trestle to discover how the situation stood.

The chums watched operations with their hearts in their mouths, figuratively speaking; but no catastrophe followed, and it began to appear that, after all, the express might pass over in safety.

Another trial was given, this time with the heavy freight engine attached to some of the largest flats, laden with steel beams. The trestle bore the strain handsomely.

"That settles it, fellows. Back to our car for us. We're going across!" sang out Jerry as he turned and made off down the track.

"How long were we here?" asked Bluff, sighing, and they knew he was thinking again of the weary hours that must elapse ere he could open that big trunk in order to ascertain whether his fears in connection with that beloved hunting-knife had any foundation or not.

"Three hours, about. Give them another half hour to get moving, and there you are. Hark! The engineer has started to whistle. That is to tell the passengers a start is intended; and here they come, rushing pell-mell, fearful of getting left." And Frank laughed at the energy displayed by some of those who had been aboard.

It was a critical time when the train slowly pushed out upon the long trestle. Everybody doubtless held their breath, and doubtless many a heart throbbed with suspense.

"It's all right, boys! We're safely over!" exclaimed Jerry, as, looking out of the open window, he could see that they had passed the critical stage.

"Oh! I'm so glad! I don't know when I've felt such a flutter about my heart. But, anyway, I secured a cracking good snapshot of that burning bridge. Every time we look at it we can remember our hold-up," observed Will, sighing with relief.

It was now about ten o'clock at night, and on account of the delay, travel was more or less congested along the line.

Frank, upon making inquiries, learned that they would not arrive at their destination until about daybreak, and so he and his chums went to their berths to secure what sleep was possible.

Frank had them up in good time, and long before dawn they were fully dressed, awaiting the arrival of the train at the valley station with impatience.

"Another hour now, and then I shall know," Bluff was saying to himself.

"Thank goodness!" exclaimed Jerry, who happened to overhear him. "And for the peace of the party, I do hope the first thing you see when you open your bag will be that awful sword."

"We're stopping, fellows!" cried Will, trembling with eagerness.

Five minutes later they jumped down from the train.

"Hello, boys! Glad to see you! Better late than never!" said a hearty voice, and then they found themselves shaking hands with a big man, whose gray-bearded face seemed to be a picture of good nature.

Of course, this was Mr. Mabie, the ranchman. He saw to it that their big trunk was dropped off the baggage car, to be seized by a couple of cowboys and hustled on to the back of a long buckboard wagon, drawn by a couple of skittish horses.

Then they were off, not five minutes after the train had pulled out.

"Here, Reddy," said Mr. Mabie to the young driver, "let me make you acquainted with some good fellows about your own age," and he introduced them one after another.

Frank saw that the cowboy was well named, for he had quite a fiery thatch; but his freckled face seemed one of the sort that invited confidence, and Frank believed he would like the other right well. Of course, Reddy was attired as all well-ordered cowboys should be. Will was secretly wild for a chance to introduce him in some picture.

"It will give such a pleasing variety to our book of views, for we haven't got a single cowboy in between the covers," he said in an aside to Frank.

They followed up the valley for over an hour. The ranch was miles removed from the railway, and surrounded by the wildest scenery the boys could remember having looked upon, and that was saying a good deal, after such a journey.

Martin Mabie was a widower, without any family. Still, he had a number of women folks on the place, a sister keeping house for him, with a Chinese cook to attend to the kitchen part of the establishment.

"Ain't this immense?" remarked Bluff, as he waited impatiently for the men to carry the big trunk indoors, so that he could satisfy his soul about the one object that had been worrying him ever since leaving Centerville.

Somehow or other they seemed slow about doing this. The horses had to be attended to first of all. Then there seemed to be some sort of excitement in the neighborhood of the corral, for the boys noticed a mounted cowboy come dashing up and jump from his steed, which was blowing hard, as if from a rapid dash.

He wondered if this sort of thing was of daily occurrence on the big ranch, which took in the whole valley for miles, and extended even up along the sides of the mountains on either hand.

"What ails the fellow, I wonder?" observed Jerry, who, it seems, had also noticed the rush of the newcomer.

"From the way he bolted into the office where Mr. Mabie went, I imagine he must have brought important news of some sort," remarked Frank.

"Perhaps our very introduction to the Big M Ranch is going to be in a whirl of excitement, fellows. I've noticed that somehow we seem to stir up things wherever we go; not that we mean to have things happen, but they just pick out such a time to play hob," said Jerry, shaking his head as if thoroughly convinced.

"Here comes Mr. Mabie, hurrying this way!" declared Bluff, beginning to forget his other anxiety for the time being in this new mystery.

"And there goes the cowboy back to the horse corral. He's shouting something, too, and as sure as you live every man is jumping to get a horse handy between his legs. Look at them slapping saddles on! Why, they'll be off like the wind! Boys, something is up! I know it!"

Frank and his chums saw several cowboys dash away as though possessed, shouting, and waving their hats in a reckless manner, as if about to charge an enemy who had designs on the cattle of the ranch.

"Whatever can it mean?" said Will again.

"For the life of me I can't imagine," returned Frank, sorely puzzled.

"But we'll soon know, fellows, for here comes Mr. Mabie, and he's swinging his hat as though just as excited as the balance of the crowd. Whatever it is, he means to tell us!" cried Jerry, his eyes glowing with the nerve-racking anxiety.

CHAPTER VII

THE GRIZZLY AT BAY

"Boys, do you want to see some fun?" called the ranchman as he came up.

"Always ready for that sort of thing, sir. What's going on?" asked Frank.

"An old friend of ours, whom we call 'Mountain Charlie,' has broken bounds at last, and is even now trying to drag one of my best yearlings off to the mountain canyon where he has his den," replied the other.

"Mountain Charlie?" repeated Frank, mystified.

"And has a den in the mountains, too! What sort of a beast is that? Or can it be a wild man?" asked Bluff.

The ranchman laughed heartily.

"I forgot you were tenderfeet, boys. We call a grizzly by that name out here. This fellow we have known for some time. Hunting him has never proven a profitable business, and, as a rule, he has never before come so far out in the open; but hunger tempted the old chap, and the man who galloped in told me he was even then dragging the yearling he had killed in the direction of the hills."

"Oh! if we could only get there in time to see them shoot him!" exclaimed Will, hitching his camera a little closer to his body.

"That's just what you're going to see. I sent word that he was not to be hurt until we arrived. Horses are being hitched up for us all. I suppose you can ride, boys?" inquired the owner of the ranch.

"To a certain extent, though I suppose your cowboys will think us pretty punky at it," answered Jerry.

"But we mean to learn everything we can while here," piped up Bluff earnestly.

"Good for you! These horses are only old plugs, however, so there's no fear of them running away with you; and here they come."

Several cowboys came toward them, each leading a number of horses. Frank thought that for "old plugs," the four intended for himself and chums possessed considerable of the fire that had animated them in other years.

"Up you go, boys. Take your pick. Then we're off."

Each seized upon the nearest animal, and, making use of the stirrup, threw himself into the saddle. As Jerry had said, all of them had frequently ridden at home, and indeed considered that they knew as much about a saddle as the average boy of the East; but that amounted to very little out here, where every one almost lived upon the back of a broncho.

"Wow! But this is going some!" said Jerry as the whole group dashed madly up the valley.

"I only hope I don't lose my camera in the rush," came from Will, who was having troubles of his own in the rear.

"Look ahead, fellows! You can see what's going on, now!" called Frank, who kept alongside the ranchman in the lead.

"Why, there's the bear, as sure as you live!" Bluff gasped.

"But what's he trying to do? First he rushes one way, and then turns around to make a bolt at the other side. He must be getting rattled."

"Don't you see, Jerry, they've got him lassoed? He wants to tackle any one of those three cowboys, but he just can't, with as many ropes pulling him in three directions."

"Talk to me about that, will you, Frank!" cried Jerry. "I never expected to see a grizzly bear held up in a rope like a steer. Look at the game little ponies on their haunches, and holding like fun. They seem somewhat scared, too, pard. Between you and me, I don't blame 'em a bit. I'd hate to think that big beast was aiming to get a grip on me."

It was just as Jerry said. The cowboys had headed the grizzly off so that he was unable to gain the safety of the wild mountain gorges. Doubtless he had been loth to leave his prey at the approach of the riders, and this had contributed to his final undoing.

One after another three of them had dropped their ropes over the head of the grizzly as he reared himself on his hind legs. The lariats stretched like piano wires under the strain, and as the cowboys had taken up positions in a sort of triangle they could keep the bear from making any sort of rush.

"Watch and see the fun," said Mr. Mabie, who had made sure to fetch his rifle along when coming from the ranch house; but he did not seem in any hurry to utilize the same.

Will, of course, immediately made good use of his camera.

Meanwhile, wilder grew the exertions of the trapped grizzly.

He was snarling with rage. The foam gathered about his mouth, and Frank shuddered as he saw the cruel teeth, not to speak of the long, deadly and poisonous claws.

"Hey, Bluff! If you only had that gentle little knife of yours handy, now would be a fine chance to rush in and have a tussle with that meek grizzly! You know you told us all just how you meant to slay the jabbercock with one straight blow."

Bluff did not make any verbal reply to this unkind thrust on the part of Jerry, but Frank, looking at him, saw that his face was deadly pale, and that he was staring at the terrible monster with whom the reckless cowboys were playing as a cat does with a mouse. He knew Bluff was feeling a chill at the thought of such a tragedy happening as his having an encounter with a beast like that.

"What if the ropes should break?" asked Frank as the captive made a more ferocious rush than usual, and the pony on the other side was dragged several feet.

"Then there would be somewhat of a mix-up, and a case of every man for himself. They'd expect me to show that I hadn't altogether forgotten my craft in connection with handling a rifle. Once I used to be a crack shot, but lack of experience plays hob with a man's nerves," replied Mr. Mabie, as he sat upon his steed and played with the repeating rifle he held.

"I see you are enjoying the situation, boys. Would one of you like to wind him up?" and the ranchman turned to Frank.

"I don't believe I would, sir," laughed that worthy.

"How about you, Jerry?"

"I've often dreamed of shooting such game, but excuse me, Mr. Mabie, it would be too much like the butcher business to please me," observed the other.

At this the stockman laughed.

"Oh, I can understand that principle of honor in a true sportsman, my lad, and I must say it does you credit; but when you come to know grizzlies better, and appreciate their terrible strength, you'll agree with the rest of us that a man has to forget such things when he gets a chance to puncture the hide of so fierce a monster as this old rogue. He could kill a horse with a single blow, or tear one into shreds with those claws. If I can get my mount to go a little closer, I'll try to wind him up with a single ball, but it's difficult to shoot from the back of a nervous pony."

He began to speak to his steed, which was striking the turf with its hoofs, and champing at the bit, as if terrified at such close proximity to, an animal so greatly to be dreaded.

Then suddenly there was a wild shout from the cowboys, and Frank, looking, saw one of them whirling his horse in wild flight, and dashing toward the group. He seemed to guess instinctively what had happened - the rope of the opposite rider must have broken under the tremendous strain. This really left the grizzly free, and, filled with mad rage, he was galloping straight toward them!

CHAPTER VIII

BLUFF MISSES SOMETHING

"Look out there!" shouted one of the cowboys.

"Run, boys!" exclaimed Frank as he started to turn his pony around so as to get beyond reach of the rapidly advancing bear.

He had just succeeded in doing this, and even started to gallop away, when he saw a sight that almost froze the blood in his veins.

Jerry had, of course, intended doing a similar vamoosing stunt. It happened, however, that his horse was more frightened than those of the others. When he jerked at the bridle the beast whirled with such a vicious fling that the boy, totally unprepared for such a move, and unable to get the grip with his knees that a cowboy always secures, went toppling over his head.

Frank, looking over his shoulder as he was borne rapidly away by his own alarmed steed, saw Jerry scramble to his knees. At any rate, he thought with relief, the other had escaped a broken neck in his ugly tumble.

Still, with that enraged grizzly bearing swiftly down upon him, in spite of the one rope that still held taut, the position of poor Jerry was not the most pleasant in the world.

Frank's first and only inspiration was to turn his horse around and rush back to the assistance of his chum. It never occurred to him that being without his own rifle, he would only be adding to the trouble by offering Bruin a double sacrifice.

His pony, however, offered serious objections to facing that roaring hurricane of a beast. Despite Frank's most strenuous efforts, he could only twist the animal's head around, but not a step would the frightened beast approach. Dancing there, he snorted his distrust and alarm.

But Frank plucked up new hope. He at the same time saw something else that gave another aspect to the case. Jerry was not to be left alone to his fate.

"Hurrah for Mr. Mabie!"

In his excitement Frank let out this shout. It was caused by seeing the ranchman leap from the back of his own horse and rapidly run back toward the spot where Jerry crouched, apparently too winded to get to his feet and try flight.

Now Mr. Mabie had reached the boy, and the barrier of his heavy repeating rifle would be between Jerry and the grizzly. Frank expected to see the stockman drop on one knee and take aim at the bear, now very close to the two dismounted ones. Nothing of the kind occurred. On the contrary, he saw Mr. Mabie thrust the rifle into the hands of the boy, who seemed to seize it eagerly.

Jerry had declined to shoot the grizzly when the beast was held by a cordon of riatas. The conditions were now considerably altered, for the huge animal was rapidly bearing down upon him, with the fire of destruction in his small, blazing eyes. It was a case of bringing his advance to a speedy stop, or suffering the consequences.

Frank's heart thrilled with pride as he saw his chum throw the rifle up to his shoulder and glance along the glistening barrel.

Mr. Mabie had shown wonderful confidence in the boy's nerve to thus place the solution of the problem in Jerry's hands.

Holding his breath, as he still tugged at the mouth of his refractory mount, Frank saw the smoke shoot out from the muzzle of the gun as the report sounded.

"Whoop! He's down!" shrieked a cowboy curveting near by.

"Take care! He's coming again, Jerry!" shouted Frank.

The bear had rolled over at the shot, but being one of the toughest animals in the world, he had immediately gained his feet again, and was once more advancing.

But Jerry knew what to do, even though he had never met quarry of this caliber before. He pumped another cartridge into the chamber, deliberately took aim, with apparently little show of excitement, and fired again.

Once more the grizzly stumbled and fell. When he tried to get up again he did not seem equal to the effort.

Mr. Mabie was shaking the hand of the young Nimrod with great enthusiasm. Perhaps he had purposely tried the nerve of Jerry, to find out what manner of boys these were, of whom old Jesse Wilcox spoke so well.

Now that the monster was dead, the ponies consented to draw somewhat closer; but the boys had to dismount, and hand over their steeds to a cowman when they wished to reach the spot where the victim of the hunt lay.

Will, with his camera, was, of course, in evidence.

"I wouldn't have missed that for a cookie!" he declared. "And if that frightened horse had only allowed me to take a crack at the time the old hermit toppled over, I'd be ever so much happier."

Frank, remembering how the other had been forced to clasp his arms around the neck of his frantic steed at the time, smiled at the impossibility of such a thing coming about.

"Give us a grip of your paw, old fellow!" cried Bluff, rushing up, brimming over with enthusiasm and admiration. "I'll sure never forget that sight! And he did the Rod, Gun and Camera Club proud when he used your weapon, didn't he, Mr. Mabie?"

"I knew he would," was the quiet remark of the stockman; and Frank understood that the other had been forming a favorable opinion of the chums from the minute he saw them come off the train.

"Would you like that skin to remember the event by, Jerry?" Mr. Mabie asked, a little later, while they were watching the cowboys remove the hide.

"It would give my mother a cold chill to see it, if she ever heard the story; but then we have a clubroom over our boathouse, and I guess it would look nice there. So, since you are so kind as to offer it, I'll say yes, Mr. Mabie."

"Well, I should remark that we'd never forgive you if you let that chance slip. It looks as though our big-game trip might pan out something worth while, after all," observed Bluff.

"You do everything on a big scale out here in the Northwest, sir. The fields of wheat are tremendous, the distances immense, the mountains higher than any in the East, by long odds; and the game the biggest in the whole country," remarked Frank.

"And in this bracing air we hope to raise the finest crop of boys in the world. But let's return to the house, lads. It's time we had a bite, for I'm sure your appetites must be sharpened by this little adventure."

The ranchman cast many a secret admiring glance toward Jerry as they rode home. He fell back with Frank on purpose to speak his mind, while the other three galloped on ahead, laughing and shouting, as boys off on a vacation always do.

"I like that chap, Jerry," he remarked earnestly. "He's a lad after my own heart. What he said about not wanting to shoot defenceless game gave me a wrench, for we cherish notions along that same line up here in the wilderness. Of course, the grizzly, as I said, does not come under that law, for he's too terrible a customer to be given much rope."

"Sometimes he takes his own rope," laughed Frank, secretly delighted to hear this honest praise of his chum.

"Which is quite true for you, Frank. That cowboy will not soon get over the humiliation of having his lariat give way. He feels very sore about it now," remarked the stockman, casting a side look toward where a couple of his herders were wrangling over something as they brought up the rear.

"I'm so glad you gave Jerry that chance. He's the most enthusiastic sportsman I ever met, and so honorable in his dealings with the wearers of fin, fur and feather. No danger of the woods ever being depopulated while he's around," Frank said, with his customary generous view of anything that concerned his chums.

"It was what you may call an inspiration. My first idea, of course, was to cover the boy and face the bear. I did not doubt my own ability to down him, but somehow I was tempted to take chances with the lad. I'm glad now I did it. He stood the racket like a veteran. I'd be a happy man if I'd only been left a boy like your chum for my own."

The ranchman spurred on ahead at this, and Frank made no effort to overtake him, for he felt sure he had seen tears glistening in the other's eyes, and could appreciate his feelings, for the stockman's only child, a boy, at that, lay with the mother in the ranch cemetery.

Breakfast was ready for them, and what a glorious meal the boys made! Just as Mr. Mabie had said, they proved as hungry as wolves. That clear mountain air seemed to tone them up after their long railway journey, and Frank laughingly declared their host had better send away for a new stock of provisions if he expected to keep them satisfied.

Bluff was the first to leave the table. Frank had seen him eating hurriedly toward the close of the meal. He knew without being told what ailed his comrade.

"He'll never be happy until he gets it, fellows!" sang out Jerry, who, of course, had also noticed the hurried departure of the anxious one.

They could hear Bluff tossing things around hurriedly in the other room, where they expected to bunk, and to which the big trunk had been finally carried.

Ten minutes later, Frank, remembering that a great silence had fallen over the neighboring apartment, stole softly to the door and looked in. He saw a picture of abject dejection there - Bluff sitting on the floor, in the midst of piles of garments, clothes bags, and all manner of things, frowning and shaking his head, as if he had lost his last friend.

"What's the matter?" demanded Frank, drawing nearer.

"Matter enough," answered the disconsolate one, sighing heavily. "Why, after all my trouble and everything, I've gone and left that knife at home, and now my whole trip is going to be spoiled for me. I just seemed to feel that something was bound to happen to upset my calculations. I might as well go back, that's what," said Bluff, gritting his teeth in his spasm of disgust.

CHAPTER IX

FRANK HAS HIS TURN

"Oh, humbug! There are other knives," remarked Frank cheerily.

"Not like that one," said Bluff dismally.

"No doubt Mr. Mabie will lend you a good one while you're here."

"Yes, he's awfully kind, but it wouldn't be that knife," groaned the bereaved Bluff.

"When do you remember seeing it last?" demanded Frank, as a suspicion darted into his brain that was connected with Jerry.

On one of their former camping trips Jerry had professed to entertain a decided antipathy toward a repeating shotgun of modern make that Bluff had bought. He declared that it was a shame for one who called himself a sportsman to handle so destructive a weapon. When a chance came, he hid the gun in a box that held some of their superfluous things. Later, upon trying to find it, in order to give it back, he learned that it was missing, and Bluff had to go without his gun until the hunt was nearly over, when it was discovered in the woods, where the thief had dropped it.

Frank wondered if Jerry was concerned in the mysterious

vanishing of the wonderful hunting-knife. He had laughed at its tremendous proportions and ornate handle. Still, it did not seem reasonable to believe that Jerry would be guilty of a second trick along those same lines.

"I was trying to remember. You know we were showing our things to the girls?"

"Yes, I believe we were," smiled Frank; for he could still see Bluff flourishing his precious knife, sheath and all, for the entertainment of Nellie.

"Well, I can't remember for the life of me seeing it again after that. You know we packed in a big hurry in the morning. I may have laid it aside, intending that it would go in on top, and then overlooked it. Such a fool play, too, when that was the prize of the whole collection!" groaned Bluff.

"And you've looked over the whole outfit here, have you?" Frank continued, surveying the piled-up mess of stuff.

"Yes; three separate times. Oh, there's no getting around it, I've made a goose of myself, and you know how I wanted to use that trusty blade so much. Of course, I won't think of moping in my tent. I'll borrow a knife, and perhaps it will do me good service; but nothing can ever take the place of that beautiful piece of steel."

"Well, let's get these things in something like order before the boys come in. Sort out what belongs to you, and chuck the balance of your extra clothes in your own bag, for I see that you've had most of them out"

"Yes. I even wondered if I could have stuck that knife in among my other shirts and underclothes, but it isn't there. I'll have to stand it, but you fellows will never know what a loss this is to me. Coming all this distance, too, just to get a chance to use it on an elk, or something worth while."

Frank thought that if Bluff had his way his mates would at least never have a chance to forget about his great loss, for he was apt to remind them of it every little while.

Will now came bustling in, anxious to ascertain if his little developing outfit came through safely, together with his packages of hypo and other necessities.

It was decided to put in that day around the ranch seeing how Mr. Mabie ran his business. Then on the following morning a party of them intended to set out for a camp in the mountains, where game would likely be found.

"We'll occupy three camps I have in view. From the first we can go to the second by taking several bullboats that will be waiting for us, and shooting the rapids in the river. That would be an experience you boys might enjoy," remarked the stockman as they rode around the valley to get a comprehensive grasp upon the way in which this enterprising settler carried on a big cattle ranch.

Reddy seemed to have been picked out by the owner to keep with them. Frank was glad of this, for somehow he had come to entertain a fancy for the smiling young cowboy.

"Rapids, did you say?" exclaimed Jerry, his face lighting up with rapture. "Why, that would tickle us from the ground up. I've always wanted to run through some little Niagara. Frank, here, has done it up in Maine, so he tells us. I hope what you have will beat his experience all hollow."

"Well, they are some rapids, I understand," replied the other, smiling.

"And if I could only be on the shore, to see you shoot down, it would afford me the greatest pleasure in the world. Not that I don't want to go through, too, but my first duty is toward securing all these wonderful events in an imperishable way by taking a picture. Some scoffers may doubt a story, but pictures never lie."

"That shows your innocence, Will," remarked Jerry. "Why, I've seen fellows standing beside the fish they caught, which I knew myself to be only ten inches long, and yet the cunning photographer had arranged it so that it looked all of two feet."

"I'm surprised that you, with all your experience, shouldn't know that," said Frank, pretending to frown.

"You mistook my meaning, that's all. What I intended to say was that *my* pictures would never lie," affirmed Will sturdily.

"Hear! hear! Somebody rub him on the back, please! But joking aside, Will, I'm ready to back you up on that score. The only fault I find with you is your ambition to take a fellow in every pickle he happens to drop into," and Jerry made a wry face as he remembered a number of scenes in which he had figured, that were wont to excite his chums to uproarious laughter at such times as they looked at the faithful reproductions in their album at the clubhouse.

In this pleasant way the day passed, and evening found them eager to complete their preparations for the morrow. Mr. Mabie answered every question fired at him by the anxious young sportsmen, especially Bluff, who wanted to know everything connected with the game they expected to hunt.

"He's trying to forget his great disappointment," said Frank as he and Jerry watched the other plying Mr. Mabie with these queries; for Bluff was the son of a lawyer, and would never take things for granted.

"What's that?" asked Jerry, for no one had been told about the loss that had come to Bluff.

"Can't find that knife of his anywhere, it seems, and believes he must have left it behind. He was looking mighty blue when I found him in the room, with all our stuff tumbled, pell-mell, out of the trunk."

Frank eyed his chum as he spoke. Jerry turned a little red.

"Not guilty, Frank! I give you my word I never touched the measly old knife. I'm sorry for him, too, for he seemed so bent on doing great stunts with it. I'll take a look myself," he said hastily, and yet meeting his chum's gaze in such a straightforward fashion that Frank never doubted his word for an instant.

"No use doing that. He rooted the whole outfit over. The knife is gone, and that's sure! I've been thinking some about it."

"And had a bright idea, I warrant. What's your solution of the mystery?"

"Why, you see, Jerry, I can clearly recollect Nellie's startled look when Bluff showed her that terribly large knife. She's afraid of such things. I'm sure she must have worried some about it, and I was thinking -"

"What?"

"That perhaps she may have considered it prudent to hide it away so that he couldn't find it again. I believe she would in my case, anyhow. It would be just like Nellie."

"Oh, well, it doesn't matter much, only Bluff is such a fellow to hang on a thing he'll never give us any peace about it. Have you asked Will?" said Jerry.

"No. I will, though; but I don't think he would bother his head about a dozen knives. If it were a camera, now, or a rapid-action rectilinear lens, you could depend on him to take notice."

Frank was as good as his word. Will denied having touched the article in question, and said he was sorry to hear Bluff would be deprived of a pleasure.

And so for the time being the mystery remained such, with Bluff occasionally digging into that trunk in a vain search, and always sighing mournfully because he failed to bring the lost treasure to light.

The boys bunked in one big room. It was very much like a picnic for them, and would often bring back pleasant memories whenever they looked at the rather clever view Will managed to get of the interior, with his chums and himself lolling there.

In the morning there was pretty much of a bustle around the ranch house.

"Ready, boys?" called Mr. Mabie, as he appeared with his gun strapped across his back, as the easiest way of carrying it.

A chorus of affirmatives greeted his question.

"Then mount, and we'll be off. They've gone on ahead last night with the tents and foodstuff, so that we'll find things in pretty much shipshape when we get on the ground."

"Say, they do things right out in this big country, eh?" said Bluff to Frank as the two of them galloped off in company.

The morning was fair and the air sharp enough to be bracing.

"Never saw anything to equal the atmosphere here," remarked Frank as their host came alongside. "There seems to be a tonic in it that even we do not have up in Maine or the Adirondacks. It makes you feel like shouting all the time."

"Everybody says the same when they first come. Presently you will grow accustomed to its invigorating tone, and quiet down. It is caused by the dry air. We are a long way from the

Atlantic, and these mighty mountains to the west act as a buffer to the moisture-laden air from the Pacific."

Crossing the valley, they were soon penetrating among the foothills at the base of the great uplifts, the tops of which bore eternal snow.

Wilder grew the scenery as they penetrated deeper into the wilderness. Frank and his chums were almost awed by the grandeur of their surroundings. At the same time, Jerry kept an eager eye on the watch for signs of game. The sportsman spirit was strong in his nature, and generally forged to the front.

It was Frank, however, who first chanced to spy something that excited his attention.

"What is that moving up yonder, Mr. Mabie? There! Look! I declare if it didn't jump straight across from that high rock to the other! Is that a Rocky Mountain sheep, sir?" he asked.

"Just what it is, my lad; and if you feel inclined, there is a chance for you to get a shot at it," came the quick reply.

"I would like it, first rate," declared Frank, immediately changing his rifle from his back to his hands.

"All right, then. Listen, and I'll tell you how it may be done. We'll rest our horses right here, for the last climb over this rough ridge to the bank of the swift river lying between. You drop down here and make your way along until you can get a chance to shoot. It will be a long shot, remember, so make allowances; and the wind is with you, not against you."

"I'll try my best, sir," said Frank, slipping off his horse.

"Be very careful as you crawl along, for a slip might cost you your life," were the last words he heard the stockman say as he began to descend the little declivity in order to make his way along its base, so as to remain concealed from the quarry.

Frank was careful as well as quick in his movements. Again and again he peeped out to see what the mountain sheep was doing. So far as he could learn, the animal seemed to be centering its attention on the caravan that had halted. Three times it moved its position, and once he was just in time to see it make a most dazzling leap, which he hoped Will might have caught with his quick-action lens.

Finally, having gained a place where he had a fine view of the animal standing there across the gorge, Frank sank down so as to get a good aim. Not quite satisfied, he crawled forward a little further, and then proceeded to put his fortune to the test.

Never had he calculated more exactly just how he should aim in order to bring the success he craved. When he pressed the trigger he was thrilled to see the mountain sheep give a wild spring into the air and then fall over the edge of the platform. This time its spring lacked the buoyancy of life, and Frank knew that his bullet had reached its billet.

But he had no time to exult, for as he moved he felt the ground slipping from under him, and realized that nothing could interpose to prevent his falling into the deep gorge!

CHAPTER X

THE YOUNG HUNTER AND THE ELK

There are times when one acts from instinct alone. Frank had no time to think, when he felt himself going down with some loose earth and stones into the wide canyon. He simply threw his rifle back of him, so that he might save it from falling, and at the same time have the free use of both hands.

He fell a dozen feet or so, along with the loose soil and rocks he had caused to give way under his weight. Then, by some happy accident, his outstretched hands closed upon a bush that was growing from the rough face of the wall, and to this he clung with desperation.

It threatened to come loose with each movement he made, and yet he was bound to find some niche for his dangling feet, so as to relieve the bush from a part of his weight.

He had heard the loud outcries of his friends, and knew they must be hastening to his relief.

If he could only hold on for five minutes all might be well.

Below lay quite an abyss, and a fall was apt to bruise him very much, even if he were fortunate enough not to have any bones broken. It was, therefore, with considerable gratitude that he discovered he could dig his toes into crevices in the rock, and thus hang on.

Jerry afterward declared that Frank presented all the appearance of a fly plastered against a wall; but it might have been noticed that he was the first one to reach the edge of the platform and breathe encouraging words to his endangered chum.

Mr. Mabie knew what would be needed before he made the first movement.

"Bring your rope, Reddy!" he shouted, and the agile cowboy had obeyed.

This was quickly lowered until the noose dangled below Frank.

"Use one foot to draw it in, my boy. We want you to get both legs inside the loop, and then gradually let us draw it up under your arms. It's all right. We're going to have you out of that, so don't worry!" called the ranchman.

"You can depend on it, Frank isn't frightened. If that bush threatens to go, get a quick grip of the rope! Do you understand, Frank?" called Jerry.

A quick nod of the head told that the one below realized he was as good as drawn up already. One foot was cautiously withdrawn from its support and the loop caught; then the second also passed inside the circle; after which a tightening of the lariat brought it up to where Mr. Mabie wanted to have it.

"Now here you come, my boy!" he called cheerily.

Frank let go his frenzied clutch, and swung into space; but willing hands quickly drew him up until he stood with his chums.

"Did I get him?" was the first question he asked, at which the stockman laughed heartily and patted him on the back.

"Spoken like a true sportsman, I declare! How about it,

Reddy?" he said.

"There's his game, sir, lying just at the foot of that old slide. It was as neat a shot as I ever saw," declared the young cowboy, pointing.

"Which is the truth, old fellow!" exclaimed Jerry, seizing Frank's hand and wringing it warmly, without a touch of jealousy, even though his own laurels as the admitted best shot of the club seemed in jeopardy.

"But what a pity we can't get it! I hate to think of killing game and leaving it for the wolves," said Frank.

"Oh, that's soon remedied. Reddy will promise to land that sheep here for you in double-quick order, eh?"

Reddy was already fastening one end of his lariat to a projecting stone that resembled a saddle-horn. This done, he tried it, to make sure that it would hold. Then he tossed the balance of the rope, loop and all, over the edge.

"Does it reach down?" asked Mr. Mabie.

"Just gets there, and no more," replied Will, craning his neck to see.

Reddy flung himself over in what struck Will as a most reckless fashion; but he discovered in time that these free riders of the ranches do everything in that nervous manner. It is a country where men quickly learn that often their lives depend on their ability to act promptly and like a flash.

"He's down already," announced Will, half a minute later.

And it was not ten minutes before they saw the cowboy coming back again. He had Frank's first mountain sheep upon his back, and though the way was rough he jumped from stone to stone with surprising agility for one who spent so much time in the saddle.

In due time the journey was resumed.

"How much further do we go?" asked Will, as he followed behind the guide, Reddy.

"Here's the top of the ridge. Now you can see the other valley, and the noise you hear is made by a cataract in the river. We camp just below that. Fishing is good there, and I guess you'll like it," was the reply.

They soon headed down, and the end of their day's work seemed close at hand. It can be easily assumed that none of the boys were sorry. Quite unused to riding, they began to feel the effects already.

"I'm glad it's a camp after this. I've sure got a cramp in my legs that it'll take a long time to get out," grunted Bluff.

"Rome wasn't built in a day, son. Each time you ride you'll notice that cramp less and less, until after a month you will be entirely free from it. But here we are at our journey's end, and I, for one, don't feel sorry, because for ten minutes I've been scenting that coffee. The boys have seen us coming, and started to have dinner cooked."

It proved to be just as Mr. Mabie said. A most appetizing camp dinner was ready for them when they arrived. Perhaps Jerry and Frank may have thought it did not fully come up to some similar feasts they had helped prepare in the woods, but of course they never hinted at such a thing; for those cowboys, while the most accommodating of fellows, were also thin-skinned in some respects.

Will was fairly delighted at the romantic looks of the camp, back of which the waterfall came tumbling down. He could hardly wait to eat his dinner before he set to work to secure a *fac-simile* of the picture, with the party gathered around the fire, and the three tents making a pleasing contrast to the dark green of the pinon trees.

Most of the party were contented to remain quiet during the balance of the day, but Bluff developed an unusually ambitious spirit for action. Truth to tell, he secretly considered that his chums were having more than their share of good luck in making a record at bagging game, and thought it time he started in.

Mr. Mabie had made him accept the use of a spare hunting-knife. It was a short, though serviceable weapon, and had doubtless done splendid execution in days gone by. Bluff used to take it out when he thought no one was looking, run his finger over the keen edge, gaze sadly at the dim blade, and shake his head. He could not get the memory of that other grand specimen of the cutler's skill out of his mind, and his soul was filled with bitterness because of its strange absence.

"Look out for wolves!" called Reddy, but Bluff only waved his hand in derision as he walked away down the valley.

Of course, he knew that the stockmen were more or less troubled with these hungry marauders in the winter time, and often had to organize grand hunts in order to keep their number down; but it hardly seemed reasonable to expect trouble from such a source in the summer season.

Elk and moose had not as yet come under the protection of the game laws, so that they were at liberty to shoot what they pleased. As a rule, however, Mr. Mabie did not believe in hunting such animals save in the fall of the year.

Bluff had asked numerous questions before leaving camp, so that he knew something about the lay of the land in the vicinity. He had started out with all due regard to the way the wind was blowing, so as not to alarm any quarry that might be sniffing up the breeze.

Climbing among the rocks, and passing through dense patches of timber, he kept on the alert for signs of game. Now, Bluff did not make any pretence at being a skilful sportsman. In fact, until a year or so back he had been the bungler of the party when it came to a knowledge of woodcraft; but since then he had studied up on various subjects, and was now anxious to air his knowledge.

When he caught sight of a large animal with towering antlers, feeding in a little glade, he knew it must, of necessity, be an elk, for a moose was built along different lines entirely.

It might have amused Jerry to see the way in which Bluff crawled closer and closer to the expected quarry. No doubt he did make some ridiculous efforts, which were not at all according to the usual rules of the game. However, as Bluff would say, the proof of the pudding lies in the eating of it, and he certainly did manage to creep up quite close to the feeding elk.

Thinking he was now near enough, and that the animal was beginning to act uneasily, Bluff stretched himself out, balanced his gun on a stone, took a long aim, and then pulled the trigger.

The elk certainly dropped, at which the young hunter gave a bellow of delight. That was where he made a foolish blunder, for believing that his bullet had done for the game, Bluff started recklessly forward, bent on bleeding the same, and only regretting the fact that he could not initiate his precious new blade.

To his astonishment, the wounded elk scrambled to its feet, and instead of bounding away it shook its antlers in an angry fashion and started straight toward the young hunter!

CHAPTER XI

THE ELK AND THE YOUNG HUNTER

"Hey! Hold on, there! That isn't in the game!"

The elk did not seem to care whether it were so or not, but came rushing straight on. Like many another, more experienced in the ways of the woods than himself, Bluff almost forgot that he had other charges in his gun. He was so amazed to see the animal he had fully believed to be dead show such surprising signs of life, that he stood there for a few precious seconds, gaping as if in a dream.

Then he made a wild spring to one side and gained the shelter of a tree.

"Oh! What a socker!" he exclaimed, as the enraged and bleeding animal came full tilt against the trunk of the tree.

Before he could say more, or try to form any plan of action, he found himself obliged to spin around that same trunk with all the rapidity he could command, for the elk was apparently determined to overtake him, and those towering antlers seemed pointed with spikes, in the eyes of the startled lad as he strained every effort to keep beyond their reach.

Bluff was really alarmed by this time. He knew that any unfortunate slip on his part would precipitate a tragedy.

"I laughed at Jerry and the wild dogs that chased him around and around, but never again for me!" he gasped, as he kept up the weary circle, hugging the trunk as closely as possible.

This, however, caused him to remember that on the other occasion his chum had finally managed to gain the victory through his own gun, and Bluff suddenly came to a knowledge of the fact that he did have a gun gripped in his hand, and which also contained five more shots.

"Hold on! Give me a breathing spell, hang you! I'll fix you yet!" he managed to exclaim, though he would better have husbanded his breath to better purpose.

The elk was not a bit accommodating. Perhaps the animal understood that so long as it kept Bluff in rapid motion the human enemy could not find a chance to use that fire-stick again, that shot out such burning missiles. At any rate, it persevered, and poor Bluff's tongue fairly hung out with fatigue.

In desperation, he was about to turn around, trusting to luck to get in a shot that would put an end to this awful chase in a circle, when the elk tripped and fell.

"Now!" gasped Bluff.

You would have thought he must have leveled his gun and fired. Jerry or Frank would, in all probability, have done that very thing. But Bluff seemed to go back to the first law of Nature, which is self-preservation.

He dropped his gun, and seizing a limb that happened to be within reach, climbed into the tree with the agility of a monkey. Fear spurred him on to do his best work just then.

"Don't you wish you could?" he shouted derisively down at the elk, which was jumping up, and making all manner of threatening movements with its antlered head, much after the fashion of an enraged goat, Bluff thought.

He was safe enough, but somehow Bluff did not like the idea of having to wait in the tree until his chums, drawn by his calls, came to the rescue. Why, he would never hear the end of the thing! It was too horrible to contemplate, and in some fashion he must secure possession of his gun to end the career of that pugnacious old bull elk.

Bluff had read more or less about the strange adventures that befall hunters of big game. He also remembered how one man had fished for his gun, and successfully, under similar conditions.

Having no cord in his pocket, he deliberately tore his handkerchief into strips and knotted them together. When this failed to reach the ground, he fastened it to the end of a long and stout "sucker," or sprout, which he cut from the body of the tree.

A running loop was made at the other end, for he could see that his gun lay in such a position that the barrel was tilted.

Bluff then began to angle. Many times he came near accomplishing his purpose, when something occurred to break up his plans.

"I'll never give up," he declared, when the elk moved forward, as if suspecting something, and endeavored to catch the dangling noose in its antlers, which Bluff would not have happen for anything.

"If I was trying to catch you, I'd want something stronger than this rag. Now please wander away again, and let me have another try," he said; and then, as the animal did walk off a dozen paces, as if encouraging him to descend, he courteously added, "Thank you."

A minute later he was thrilled to find that his erratic loop had actually dropped over the end of the gun barrel. A quick jerk at the proper instant tightened the clutch, and after that it was the easiest thing in the world to pull the weapon up within reach of his trembling hands.

"Now, we'll see if you're going to have the laugh on me, you old scamp! Hi! Hold on, there! Who said you could walk away? Come back here, and have it out! I dare you!"

The elk, as if suspecting that all was not well, had indeed started to move off. But when Bluff made a great feint of coming down, he succeeded in exciting the animal's anger again, and caution was flung to the winds.

Bluff watched for his chance, and when it came he made sure work of it by sending a bullet through the heart of the fighting elk.

Even then he waited a little while.

"Going to try getting up again? This time I'm ready for you, old fellow!" he said to the fallen beast; but presently it became patent, even to his inexperienced eyes, that the elk had breathed its last.

"Now, if Will were only here," Bluff remarked enviously, as he put one foot on his prize and tried to look very unconcerned, as if knocking down such big game might be a matter of almost daily occurrence with him.

Not knowing how to go about cutting the elk up, Bluff headed back toward the camp. Before leaving the spot he thought to bleed the quarry, after a fashion, for he understood that such a thing was always done to make the meat taste better.

Half an hour later he showed up in the camp. It was next to impossible to get lost in that valley, which might account for Bluff finding his way back with comparative ease.

Jerry was lounging alongside one of the tents, engaged in getting his fishing tackle in order, for a try in the pool below the falls.

"Shall we send the horses out to tote it in?" he asked, after the usual fashion of greeting greenhorns when they come back from a hunt apparently unattended by success.

"Did you hear me shoot?" asked Bluff carelessly.

"Why, yes, twice; and some time apart. What was it - a crow or a jack-rabbit?"

Bluff only smiled as Mr. Mabie came out of the tent and glanced at him.

"What would you say that was, sir?" he asked, thrusting something in front of the old stockman.

Starting back, Mr. Mabie looked hastily at the hairy object.

"An elk's tail, as sure as you live!" he remarked, his face relaxing in a smile.

"What's that?" roared Jerry, springing to his feet.

"Oh, you needn't get excited about it. Do you see the dull spots on my knife? Well, I bled my game, all right, just as I wanted to do with that bully good blade that was left behind; and if Reddy will only go back with me, we can bring the old fellow in on a horse," said Bluff coolly.

"Count me in on that!" exclaimed Will, rushing out of his impromptu dark-room, and waving the bottle in which he was making a solution of hypo.

"I think I'll go along, too," remarked Frank, appearing from some other place.

When the party started forth presently, there were six of them with the horse - the chums, Reddy, and Mr. Mabie himself.

"I am beginning to believe you boys will corral everything in sight if you keep on the way you've started. A grizzly, a sheep, and now an elk; and only thirty hours with me! H'm! Perhaps I may not be able to show you as much about big-game hunting as I expected," said the stockman, who seemed vastly amused at the energy shown by his young guests at the ranch.

"Oh, we can pull a trigger, all right, sir, but there are a thousand things we want to know about these natives that books never teach. I'm like a sponge, and can keep on soaking up information all the time," laughed Frank.

Incautiously, Bluff let fall certain words that gave Jerry a clue as to the true situation.

"A tree! Shot him downward from a tree, eh? Now, since you've so frankly confessed that much, why not tell the whole blooming story, Bluff?" he cried.

"There isn't much to it. I saw the elk. Then I shot him, and he fell over. After that the elk saw me. He chased me about a tree. I remembered how fast Jerry said he ran around when those wild dogs were after him, and I wanted to go him just one better. Then I found a chance to climb when the wounded elk stumbled. After that I made a rope out of my handkerchief and fished with a loop until I caught the barrel of my gun. That's all."

"A whole history in a nutshell. But we must be getting near the place, according to what you said at the start. There are the three oaks growing in a clump. Now where's your dead elk?"

As Frank spoke he turned to Bluff. That individual was staring around in evident bewilderment.

"It was sure here I met him. There's the little glade, and this big tree is the one I climbed up into. I saw him lying there. I *know* he was dead when I bled him. But I must be blind, for the elk certainly is not here now. Oh! Did he come to life again, and run away?" said poor Bluff, in despair, looking at the tail, which he had thrust into his belt.

CHAPTER XII

HARD LUCK

"Talk to me about your dreamers!" muttered Jerry, shrugging his shoulders.

"But I tell you it was so!" asserted Bluff, firing up.

"The boy is right," said Mr. Mabie, as he stepped forward and fastened his eyes upon the ground.

Frank saw immediately what the stockman had in mind. These things mentioned by Bluff could never have happened without leaving some tangible traces behind. Where a big elk had been slain there must be signs of the blood that had flowed.

"Look here, and see for yourself, Jerry." And Mr. Mabie pointed to the ground at his feet.

"There's some marks of hoofs around, I admit, and they seem to circle about the tree, just as Bluff says; and - yes, that's blood on the ground, as sure as you live! I guess I'm on the wrong track. He did have a merry circus. He did shoot an elk, but where has the blooming thing gone?" exclaimed the scoffer.

"That's just what I'm going to find out through Reddy, here. He has some local reputation as a tracker. Put your nose down to it, and let us know what happened, Reddy."

In accordance with the request of the ranchman, the cowboy threw himself upon his hands and knees.

"Indians!" he announced, before they had taken half a dozen breaths.

"What?" cried Bluff, staring hard.

"Cree Indians been here. I can see the print of their moccasins plain as day; and here's where they dragged the elk along, heading toward the river!"

Reddy seemed to have not the slightest trouble in reading the signs, and yet to the boys there was not the faintest vestige of marks. Presently, however, Frank was able to make out the print of a foot in the soil, and he noted that the one who made it wore no heels. His footwear must be moccasins.

"H'm!" remarked Mr. Mabie. "Just what I suspected. The thieving Crees have robbed our young friend of his prize. Too bad! But there are more elk around, Bluff, and I hope you'll have other chances."

"But that one chased me so hard I wanted revenge. I calculated on eating a bit of his flank for my dinner. What's the matter with our following up the scamps, and making them give up some of my game, anyhow?" demanded the disappointed hunter.

"Impossible just now. The river is close by, and they undoubtedly had boats in which they fled, carrying off your elk. By this time they've shot the rapids, and must be miles below. Possibly we may run across the rascals later, when we also go down the river," replied Mr. Mabie.

Reddy had gone off, his head bent low, and they understood that he was following the trail, much as a hound would have done, with this one difference, that whereas a dog pursues by scent alone, the cowboy had to depend on his eyes.

"But if game is so plentiful, why should these Crees want to steal my elk?" pursued Bluff, who could not be easily satisfied.

"That bothers me to answer. Perhaps they happened to be out of ammunition. There are several other explanations, but in my opinion the most probable is the natural meanness of certain dusky bucks; just as your able tramp refuses to do a lick of work, while he'll walk twenty miles for nothing," smiled the other.

"There comes Reddy back. Perhaps he knows more about it now," said Frank, who was decidedly interested in the enigma.

They waited until the cowboy joined the circle about the tree.

"Boats, Reddy?" asked Mr. Mabie.

"Three. Must have carried around the falls without our knowing it. Hung about here, waiting to steal something from our camp. Had a snare set for jack-rabbits. Saw some torn skins in the camp," was what the cowboy replied, in his jerky way.

"Oh! Then I guess they must have been here before we came, and all you say makes me believe I was right. They have no arms, or else their powder and shot have run out; and for some reason they are afraid to meet whites. Well, the elk's gone, and we can't mend that. Let's return to camp. You have the tail to show for your little adventure, my lad."

"Yes, sir; and the memory of it all, which will haunt me for a good long time," said Bluff, with a shake of his head, as he contemplated the historic tree around which he had done a little Marathon.

"But I mean to get a picture of this tree, anyhow, just to remind Bluff how valuable a good pair of sprinting legs may be sometimes," laughed Will.

And he did, with Bluff standing alongside; for once the official photographer demanded a pose, he was bound to get it, or throw up his job, for such was the law of the Rod, Gun and Camera Club.

Then they retraced their steps to the camp, Frank more than usually thoughtful, for anything in the shape of a mystery always set him to puzzling, and he more than once wondered whether they would ever learn just why those Crees stole the elk Bluff had downed after so much trouble.

"How many did there seem to be?" he asked Reddy, a little later.

"You mean of the thieving reds? I counted nine in all, four bucks, two squaws and three pappooses," replied the other.

"But if I understand rightly, these Indians never take their families when they go on the war-path. Is that so, Reddy?" Frank asked quickly.

"Say, get that notion out of your head right away. They ain't no Crees lookin' for trouble these days. My idea is just this: This is a family travelin' acrost country, for some reason or other. P'raps they got kicked out of their pesky old village. I've knowed such things to happen. Then they run short of meat, and didn't have guns or powder. Under such conditions any redman would steal."

"Well, who could blame them, with women and children to feed? I guess you hit the nail on the head that time, Reddy. Glad to think that way, too. We can spare the elk, and it will spur Bluff on to other hunting deeds. He's had a taste now, and the fever will work on him."

Meanwhile, Jerry had started his fishing below the cataract. There were places just at the end of the foam-splashed outlet of the big pool where they had seen noble trout jumping, and it was here he dropped his flies.

After trying them a short time, and ascertaining that the trout paid little attention to the feathery lure, practical Jerry actually descended to the plebian angleworm, though he blushed when Frank came over to watch him.

"Got to have some for supper, you know," he remarked. "Now, if I was only doing this thing for the sport, nothing could tempt me to use live bait. I'm at it in the strict commercial sense this time."

"I understand; and Jerry, let me tell you, the sportsman who, when trout-hungry, refuses to go back to first principles, and use grubs and worms after the fish refuse the fly, is to be pitied, that's all," laughed Frank.

"Hey! That's a dandy, all right! See him jump, will you? Wow! He's all of two pounds, and as strong as an ox! I hope the leader holds. It's been frayed some by rubbing over rocks in the past. Please pick up that landing-net and attend to the beauty, if I can coax him close enough, Frank."

Frank landed not only that beauty, but several more, ere he wandered off to do something else. Jerry kept on fishing until he could not get another bite, by which time he had quite a nice string of the speckled beauties.

"Perhaps enough for a decent meal; though if Bluff develops his usual appetite, the rest of us would go hungry. I wonder if a fellow mightn't have some luck up above the falls? Guess I'll make a shift to try," he said to himself.

The last view he had of the camp showed him Reddy amusing Bluff by making flying tosses of his rope and lassoing all sorts of objects, from the hat on the head of the admiring witness, to something tossed up in the air.

Jerry labored up the hillside until he finally came to where he could look down at the water as it shot over the edge. It fell with a great deal of noise, striking the rocks below in many places with terrific force.

"Ugh! It would just about bang a fellow to pieces to drop over there," he remarked, commencing to move upstream, looking for a promising place to begin his fishing operations.

Presently he discovered a log that jutted out over the swift current. From this outlook he believed he could allow his bait to float down into an eddy that looked as though it might be the home of a big hermit trout.

Jerry tested the log as he cautiously advanced. He realized that he was taking some chances in creeping out to its furthest end, but so far as he could ascertain it seemed to be firm enough.

Straddling the log, he started to get his baited hook in motion. The wriggling worms sank a little in the swirl. At first, he was unable to just master the difficult problem of how to influence the bait to float into the eddy. Twice he failed to accomplish this, but studying the rushing stream a little, he fancied that by a certain throw in the start he could gain his end.

Sure enough, it worked, and like a charm. The baited hook was drawn back into the foam-flecked eddy, and he saw it vanish from view. Then came a most tremendous jerk, that almost caused him to lose his balance and the log to quiver, with sickening possibilities.

But Jerry glued his legs against the sides, just as he had been told to do with a refractory pony, and managed to recover his balance. The trout was a gamey one, and the swiftness of the current made the task of securing him doubly hard.

"I'll work, all right, for everything I hook here," panted Jerry, after ten minutes had passed, and he tossed his exhausted prize over to the bank.

But he would not give up. Where one such fine, fat fellow held out there was certainly a chance for more, so he continued his fishing.

Unknown to him, Will had also wandered up that steep hillside, searching for a new view of the wonderful cataract. Pushing through the dense thickets, he chanced to catch a glimpse of the lone fisherman.

"Now, that's what I call a picturesque sight! Look at the chap perched out on the very end of that log, with the water rushing below like a mill-race! Here's where I get you, my duck. Fancy to what ends a fisherman will go in order to enjoy his favorite sport."

Will seemed to forget entirely that he was willing to undertake just as long a pilgrimage and buck up against as difficult problems simply to get one snapshot that appealed to his soul.

"There! He's got another fish on! My! How it pulls! I wouldn't be out on that log, doing such a job, for anything. But I just bet Jerry is as happy as a clam. He sets his teeth, and holds on as if he had a whale, and perhaps it is a big un! I must get him again in that position. Why, although he don't know it, he's just giving me the best thing of the day!"

Will rapidly adjusted his camera, and looked down to see that he had the proper focus before snapping the shutter. The light was good up there, and he believed he must have the greatest success with such a picture as that. Besides, it had the genuine article of life in it, which he always sought in taking his views.

Then he pressed his finger, in the belief that he was about to snatch a snapshot bound to give the four chums the keenest satisfaction in days to come.

"Oh!"

The startled exclamation broke involuntarily from the lips of Will even at the very second he took his picture, and he let his beloved camera fall to the ground, at the risk of doing it some material damage.

It was not this seeming mishap that had brought the startled cry from his lips, but the crash of sundering wood, and the sudden disappearance of the lone fisherman below the rim of the river bank; for the log had finally betrayed Jerry, and dropped him into that swirling, maddening current above the high falls!

CHAPTER XIII

AN INVADER IN CAMP

Will dashed madly toward the river bank. It happened that he was somewhat below the point where Jerry's mishap had come about. Hence, he was able to reach the edge of the stream in a dozen seconds.

Even that short time had been enough to sweep the imperiled lad past the place. Will was thrilled with horror to see his chum in the midst of the churning current, trying to cling to a slippery rock, from which insecure hold he was being gradually but surely sucked by the fierce power exerted by the rushing stream.

Never had the roar of the falls sounded more terrible to poor Will than when he saw Jerry suspended, as it were, above the great drop. Once he lost his hold, he must be swept irresistibly over the edge, down to those cruel rocks below.

Will would have foolishly attempted to reach his chum had he chanced to be opposite the place where Jerry hung on with the desperation of despair. As it was, he could do nothing, which was just as well, for there must only have been two of them given over to the river once he ventured into that mill-race.

"Help! Oh, help!" he shrieked.

The roar of the cataract must have muffled his call, so that it might just as well have been a whisper.

Just as Will was about to give up in despair, and count Jerry as good as lost, he made a sudden discovery. Another figure had appeared on the bank, and just at a point opposite the rock to which Jerry clung.

"Reddy! Save him! save him!" cried Will, wringing his hands.

Then he became mute with suspense. The cowboy did not recklessly rush into the boiling flood, for he knew only too well that such a course could not help the imperiled one. Instead, Will saw him whirling his rope about his head with lightning-like haste.

His heart in his eyes, Will continued to stare, holding his very breath. He saw the coils of rope fly out just as when Reddy was giving his exhibition in camp. Not far did they have to speed, for Jerry was close to the shore.

"Oh! what luck! He's done it! He's done it! Jerry has the rope now, and he is coming in, hand over hand! Bully! bully! bully!"

Will was so excited that he fairly danced up and down as he shouted these words aloud. Then, bethinking himself of what a magnificent picture he was losing, he took several steps in the direction of the spot where his camera lay. Stopping hastily, as his affection for his chum more than counterbalanced his love for an effective scene, he turned around and hurried to join the others.

Jerry was ashore, and wringing the hand of Reddy, when Will arrived.

Regardless of the rescued boy's wet clothes, Will threw his arms around him.

"Oh! you gave me such a fright, Jerry! I'm quivering all over! How lucky Reddy happened to be here, and with his rope, too!" After saying which he turned his attention to the smiling cowboy, and squeezed his hand ardently.

"I sure beat my record that time, boys. I've roped some queer things, but never a feller that was going whoopin' over a falls. Don't know why I slung the old lariat over my arm when I started up here to see what luck Jerry had. Mighty glad now I did, though. It'd been purty hard to get him out with only a stick to stretch over."

Reddy was extremely modest, and only too willingly agreed not to say a word about the mishap and rescue to any of the others; and Will was also bound to secrecy by Jerry.

Back in the woods they made a fire, where Jerry succeeded in drying his clothes.

"Anyhow, I saved that fish," he announced, with a satisfied shake of the head.

Will looked at the cowboy inquiringly.

"Sure thing he did. When he came ashore he had that line fast in his hand, and pulled the trout in before he'd even shake. He's a real sport, all right," said Reddy, with admiration in his manner.

"It seems as though these things are born in one. Now, I'd have dropped my rod the very first thing, and howled for help," remarked Will.

"How about your camera?" asked Jerry wickedly.

"H'm! That's a different thing. But when I saw you go in I did let that fall. Luckily, no damage was done. My heart would be broken if the blessed little black box got out of shape. But I've one picture of you on that log," announced Will.

"And that will be enough to give me a clammy feeling every

time I look at it," nodded Jerry, who was in secret more shaken by his recent terrible experience than he cared to show.

They went down a little later, Jerry carrying his two dearly-earned trout. And when the others praised the fisherman that evening at supper for supplying their camp table, they little dreamed how near their hard-working chum had come to disaster in his efforts to land the enticing finny beauties of the river.

Besides the trout, they enjoyed mutton that night, for Frank's mountain sheep was brought into use. Perhaps it was tough, perhaps the flavor did not strike the boys quite as favorably as some mutton they had eaten at home, but such trifles could not dampen their enthusiasm a particle, and they voted the meal a grand success all around.

Seated about the blaze afterward, they chatted until late. Bluff was inclined to be a bit moody, and sat by himself, listening to all that was said, but taking no share in the conversation.

Frank noticed that he seemed to fondle his rifle more than usual, and he believed the other must be thinking of the elk he had shot, but which had been stolen by those wandering thieves of Crees.

"He's still worrying about that butcher knife of his," whispered Jerry, nudging Frank as he spoke. "I wonder will the fellow ever forget it?"

"Now, I was watching him, and, to tell the truth, I fancy Bluff has become aroused to the delight of bringing down big game. That elk was a revelation to him. See how he listens while Billy is telling of the panther tracks he saw not a great way off. I wouldn't put it past Bluff to aspire to knocking over a panther if the chance ever came his way.

"Huh! I hope he is lucky enough to get a fatal shot in, then; for one of those gentry is apt to maul a fellow good and hard if only wounded. Billy has been telling of some fierce times he's had with the beasts. His arms are all scarred up from deep cuts made by the claws of a panther years ago," remarked Jerry.

"Whew! Hear what he says? will you?" remarked Frank.

"Why, yes, kid," observed the old cowboy, in answer to a question Bluff had put, "sometimes I've knowed 'em to jump into a camp and snatch the meat right from under the nose of a feller. Let a painter git good an' hungry, an' he ain't afraid of anythin' but fire. Then, ag'in, I've knowed 'em to act as cowardly as coyotes. I kinder reckon the season has considerable to do with their actin'."

"But that was only one man. The beast wouldn't dare jump in a camp like this, no matter how hungry he might be?" continued Bluff, who seemed strangely interested in the subject, Frank thought.

The old cowpuncher laughed as though amused.

"That's somethin' I'd hate to commit myself on, younker. All I say is a painter ain't to be depended on. He might prove a coward, like some cats, and again you'd be fair astonished at his darin'. Long ago I made up my mind never to give him more of a chance than I could help. It's war to the knife between me and any such prowlin' critter. I can't git my gun workin' too quick to please me when I sees the yaller eyes of a painter hoverin' round my camp."

"Are their eyes always yellow?" asked Bluff eagerly.

"I reckons they are, kid; leastways all that I ever see was marked that way," replied the cowboy, reaching out for a brand with which to light the cigarette he had been rolling between his fingers, just as Reddy was also doing at the time.

"Like those yonder, do you mean?" said Bluff, pointing behind Billy, to a point where the dense thicket came close to the border of the camp.

Every eye was instantly turned in that direction. Frank himself was thrilled when he discovered that there were twin glowing eyes among those bushes, eyes that had all the attributes of the cat tribe.

Various exclamations arose from the group.

"By gum! It's a painter, sure as you live!" said Billy calmly.

"Never heard of one so bold!" whispered Reddy hoarsely, feeling for the weapon he usually carried attached to his belt.

"Everybody sit quiet, and see what he means to do. He won't attack us, but it may be you'll see him make a jump for the balance of that sheep over yonder. The scent of the game has aroused his hunger. Look at him raise his head to see!"

Mr. Mabie spoke these words in a low but tense tone. He was more or less excited by the strange actions of the prowling panther.

"I reckon it's a mother, with hungry cubs near by. She's just bound to get some grub for the kits, men or no men. Now, if you lie low, and watch, I reckon you'll see something you never expected to see in your born days."

Billy sat there motionless. Only Frank saw the movement of Bluff when he raised his rifle, and while he would have warned his chum against the folly of firing, before he could frame words to carry his meaning, the quick report came, causing a sensation among those around the fire.

The crouching beast, infuriated by receiving a sudden, painful wound, launched straight out, and landed in the midst of the campers!

CHAPTER XIV

THE COWBOY GUIDE

Everybody was in motion at once.

Some went over backward, regardless of appearances; others rolled aside, bent upon placing some little distance between themselves and the invader. Bluff was trying to work the mechanism of his gun in order to secure a second shot, but as so often happens when the hunter is excited, he failed to accomplish what should have been an easy change.

The maddened panther had crouched again after landing close to the fire. Perhaps what acted more than anything else to keep the beast from leaping once more was the uncertainty of choosing among so many which he should attack. If he only knew from whence had come that sting which had given him such sudden agony there would have been no hesitation at all.

One, however, did not join in the almost universal retreat. This man was Reddy. He had been leaning forward at the time, as stated, about to pick up a brand with which to light his cigarette. Some impulse urged him to seize a flaming, heavy stick that stuck out of the fire, and make a frantic attack upon the crouching panther.

Frank never forgot that spectacle. The panther, with ears flattened back, and fangs exposed, snarled and carried on just like a big house cat when assailed by a small but saucy dog, striking out from time to time, as though trying to reach the arm that wielded the cudgel.

The flaming brand caused too much fear to allow of an attack. Still, the ugly beast would not give way, and leap out of its perilous position.

"Where's my gun?" At least three different shouts arose.

"Get out of range there, kid!" bellowed Billy, who had drawn a heavy revolver, and, on hands and knees, sought to get a line on the common enemy.

"But that's my panther!" cried the voice of Bluff.

Frank saw him once more bring his rifle up to his shoulder. Although hardly in a position to see what was going on, Will seemed to be fumbling with something in a desperate fashion. The fellow, as usual, was thinking only of what a grand thing it would be if he could only get that scene for posterity to gaze upon.

"I hope Bluff aims straight!" Frank was saying to himself, for he knew there was more or less danger of the bullet doing some damage to one of the campers who might happen to be on the other side, partly screened by the brush.

The crash of the gun followed.

"Wow!" shouted Reddy, falling back as the panther tumbled over in his direction, for he knew what damage those poisonous claws might do in the dying agony of the beast.

Then the rest of the scattered company appeared. Some crawled out from the brush, others arose from flattening themselves on the ground, while still another group made their exit from under the canvas of the tent close by.

The beast was writhing in its last hold on life.

"That's my panther, I told you!" said Bluff, jumping to his feet, and still holding on to his gun.

He was as white as a ghost, but a fire shone in his eyes telling of the spirit that had finally been aroused there. Jerry would soon have to look to his laurels now.

Mr. Mabie laughed as he patted Bluff on the back.

"I reckon it is, youngster; but you took big chances that time. I'd advise you to slow up a bit in the future, when shooting in the dark. That impetuous nature will sure get you into more than one scrape, otherwise," he said soberly.

Bluff hung his head. He knew now that he had been too hasty, when there were so many older campaigners than himself around; but the loss of that elk had rankled in his heart, so that he could not resist the sudden temptation to redeem his reputation.

Jerry, for once, had nothing to say, at least to the successful one. He bent over the dead panther, and examined it with curiosity. Will was loudly lamenting the fact that once again he had found himself left in the lurch.

"You fellows move too fast," he declared. "Now, if Bluff hadn't put in his oar, I was just about ready to shoot off a flashlight picture. Just think what it would mean to see Reddy, here, banging that big cat over the head with his torch! Oh! it's just too mean for any use! Everything goes wrong just when I'm going to squeeze my bulb, and get the best picture there ever was! Even a rotten old log has to go and break off short -"

"Hey, Will! Let up on that whining, won't you?" cried Jerry, just then, fearful lest his secret was about to come out.

Frank looked suspiciously at both his chums. Perhaps he may have entertained a dim thought that there was something between them that they did not want known; but other things soon put this out of his mind for the time being.

"We must keep an eye out the rest of the time we're here," said Billy, after the company had settled down again around the fire.

"Why?" asked Bluff, looking up from admiring the sleek fur of his prize.

"The brutes often hunt in couples, you know. This was the mother, just as I had an ijee, and she's got half-grown cubs around somewhere. If the mate's near by he may give us a call sooner or later."

Bluff's hand had stolen out toward his gun at these words.

"Here! No more of that, my lad!" said Mr. Mabie. "You've had your fling, and come out of it mighty lucky. Don't try it again while I'm around, please. If any more uninvited visitors drop in, you leave them to the rest of us."

But there was no further alarm. During the night some of them declared they heard strange cries off in the woods, which Mr. Mabie said must have been the whining of the panther cubs, looking in vain for their mother.

Frank was distressed.

"I hope they're really big enough to forage for themselves. If there's anything I dislike it's to shoot bird or beast that has young depending upon it. Perhaps the old male may look after them," he suggested.

"Well," smiled Mr. Mabie, "I hardly think that will prove to be the case; at least they don't, as a rule. But I've got an idea the cubs are of a good size, and can find some means of subsisting. For my part, I wouldn't care if every panther in the Northwest were rubbed out. I've no love for the sly beasts. They've robbed me of more than one fine calf, I can tell you."

After breakfast a hunt was organized.

"We ought to get an elk before leaving up here," said the stockman as they prepared to go forth again in a squad; "and as this will be our last day in camp by the falls, we must look sharp."

"Then we make tracks to-morrow?" asked Frank.

"Hardly that, since we go by water. You've seen the three bullboats yonder. We send our tents and all other things around with the horses, while we shoot the rapids, and enjoy the most exhilarating boat ride you ever dreamed of. Just wait and see, boys. It will be something worth while."

After all, the stockman was unable to start out with them. He was subject to attacks of rheumatism, due to his age, and many exposures in the past. When one of these came on Mr. Mabie was unable to walk any distance, and, unfortunately, he experienced such an attack that morning.

"Sorry, boys, but it can't be helped. Reddy, here, will have to take my place. You don't need me, that's plain. Only don't be too reckless, now. That's the fault with most youngsters," and he shook his head at Bluff, who turned fiery red as his eyes fell upon the panther, which Billy was skinning at that moment.

Of course, Reddy was to act as guide to the party. He had been around the vicinity a number of times. Besides, he knew the habits of the elk, which used this valley for their feeding grounds, and if any one could lead them to success in their hunt it was the young cowboy.

Frank used to look at Reddy, and wonder if he had ever seen him before; but as that was out of the question, he came to the belief that it was simply a matter of resemblance.

"Look there!" exclaimed the guide, before they had gone two hundred steps from the camp, and pointing as he spoke.

"What was it?" asked Jerry eagerly.

"I saw a gray critter slinking away into that thicket!"

"The panther's mate!" cried Bluff excitedly, as he fingered his gun.

"I reckon it was; but we ain't lost no panther, and anyhow, this is a hunt for elk meat. Come along, boys," remarked Reddy hastily.

They tramped for half an hour steadily, going far beyond where Bluff had had his strange adventure with the wounded elk. Will trailed along in the rear, holding on to his beloved camera. The woods looked as though the recent dry weather had seared the leaves more or less, but they lacked the splendid gorgeous tints of autumn.

More than once the others had to wait for the straggler, or else call to him. He grew so interested in his surroundings, especially when trying to get a view that particularly appealed to his fancy, that he was apt to forget their mission entirely.

Once he aroused himself to the fact that he could no longer see his comrades, or catch a sound of their voices. This disagreeable idea caused him to hurry, and no doubt he became less cautious in navigating some of the various narrow paths, for before he realized that he had started a small avalanche, he was caught up in its gathering swoop, and found himself being carried swiftly down a rather steep declivity, unable to stay his rush.

CHAPTER XV

IN THE RAPIDS

"Give him another call, Frank!"

"That fellow beats all creation for lagging! I believe he'd rather snap off his old camera than eat, any day. If he doesn't look out, that panther may get - Glory to goodness! What's that, Reddy?" cried Jerry.

"Sounds like a bit of an avalanche, though this here is a queer time of year for that. Generally comes, you know, in snow time, or when the rains arrive," was the cowboy's ready answer.

"But - Will - he may have started it, and gone down into one of these beastly holes!" observed Bluff uneasily.

"Let's go back, fellows, and make sure," remarked Frank instantly.

They retraced their steps, Reddy leading the way, and every one on the lookout for any signs of an unusual happening.

"There's where it fell, and it looks like quite a lot of stuff had gone down the slope," said their guide presently.

"Hello, Will! Will!" shouted Frank.

"Well, I'm waiting for you," said a quiet voice close at hand.

"Where in the world are you, pard?" burst out Jerry.

"Oh, here," came the reply.

"Ginger! I believe he's down the bank!" cried Bluff.

"Just what he is! Come here, fellows! Did you ever see anything to beat that? Talk to me about your lucky dogs! Here's one that takes the cake every time!" sang out Jerry, as he thrust his head out beyond the edge of the platform where the slope began.

"Oh, I don't know. There have been cases where people have been saved from all sorts of disasters by the fortunate presence of a rope. Chuck us a loop, Reddy, will you, please?" said Will, and Jerry became as dumb as an oyster.

No wonder Frank laughed, even while he watched the cowboy dropping his lariat down as the other so coolly requested. Will had slid some twenty feet down the steep bank, along with the loose surface stuff, which gathered force as it proceeded. Then a projecting stone had caught the bag of his coat, and he was supported in this fashion by the stout fabric.

"What are you trying to do down there? Expect to cut me out of my job as the cliff climber of the party?" asked Frank jokingly.

"Not so that you'd notice. Thought I might get a better view down along here. But first of all, save my precious camera, before I consent to come up," answered Will, and he insisted upon fastening the same to the dangling rope.

Bluff saw his chance to get back at his chum for more than one indignity along the same line that he had suffered in the past, so he called out:

"Here, you! Just hold your horses! I'm going over yonder and strike you off as you hang there. It will do to amuse the girls when we get home. We don't often have a chance to bring the photographer into these pictures. Now, here you are. Look pleasant! There! That job's done! Now yank him up, fellows, and don't be too easy with him. He deserves a good digging for scaring us so."

But Will had suffered no material harm from his little slide.

"Glad I stopped part way," he observed, looking down, "for it's quite some distance to the bottom, and then those rocks would have bruised me more than a little. Yes, I agree with Bluff, there; it's better to be born lucky than rich."

After that they saw to it that Will did not lag behind. He was not to be trusted any more than could be helped.

Reddy was as good as his word. He eventually brought them within sight of several feeding elk. They carried out his further directions to the letter, and were thus enabled to approach within easy gunshot of the unsuspicious animals.

A program had been arranged, and every one knew just what part in it he was expected to play. Consequently, there was no confusion. Frank, Jerry and Bluff had their chance to aim. To each was assigned a different quarry, though after the first shot they were to fire as they pleased.

"Ready?" whispered the master of ceremonies, after Will had performed his little, necessary operation with his camera that would produce happy results.

"Yes," said Frank.

"Ditto!" from Jerry.

"Same here," came from Bluff.

"Then go!"

There followed a crash of firearms. Instantly confusion broke out among the little herd of feeding elk. One was down, another went limping off, to fall as Frank sent in a second hasty shot; while the balance fairly flew off in their fright.

"Hurrah!" shouted the hunters, as they saw that they had met with splendid success, since two of the big animals had fallen to their guns.

Bluff looked grimly disappointed.

"I hit my buck, for I saw him go down on his knees," he asserted moodily.

"Oh, that ain't anything. An elk often runs off with several bad wounds. I only hope he don't die in the woods somewhere," said Reddy, examining the tracks of those that had escaped.

"Will it pay us to follow them up and see if Bluff's buck fell?" asked Frank, more to please his chum than because they needed the game.

"Nope. The buck runs like he wasn't even hurt much. No ketchin' up with them fellers after that riot call. We'd best pay attention to what we've got, and return to camp," replied the guide; and Bluff shrugged his shoulders, saying:

"But I hit him, anyhow, I'll tell you that, fellows."

Frank found that all Reddy meant to do was to hang the two elk up, after they had cut some choice portions for immediate use. The other cowboys would come with the horses, on their way down the river, on the morrow, and secure the game.

"We got fooled out of elk steaks once and don't mean to again, I tell you," said Jerry, as he shouldered his portion of the load.

So they returned to camp.

"What's this?" said Mr. Mabie as they came filing in. "Back already, and only out two hours? Got some meat, too, I see. That's good. Such appetites as you boys are developing threaten to eat us out of house and home soon, unless we eke out with game. Who cut up the elk?"

"The boys all took a hand. They wanted to learn," smiled Reddy.

"I kind of thought they had," nodded the stockman, who could easily see that it was not the work of an experienced hand.

Bluff failed to catch the twinkle of humor in the other's eyes.

"Yes, and I could have made even a better job if I'd had the knife along I foolishly went and left at home," he remarked disconsolately, whereat Jerry, Will and Frank exchanged looks, and shrugged their shoulders, but said nothing; for in a case of that kind words are useless.

They were all very enthusiastic that night over the feast. The cook had dutifully pounded the steaks before placing the same on the fire, so that if they seemed tough it was not his fault.

The meat, however, was sweet and tasty; and besides, with hunger serving as the best-known sauce, who could complain?

Bluff kept on the lookout for the mate of his panther, but if the old fellow was prowling around he had more discretion than to show himself while these hunters were near by.

With the morning the camp was to be abandoned. Tents came down while they were eating breakfast, and everything was packed away in as small a compass as possible, for carrying on the backs of the pack horses, which were brought in from the pen, or corral, where they had been kept all this while, in charge of a guard.

The three bullboats awaited the adventurous ones. These were of the type much used in this far region of the Northwest, being fashioned of tough hides of bulls, and impervious to water.

Besides their guns, which were strapped to their backs, the voyagers carried little or nothing. In case of an upset they did not stand to worry over anything except saving their own lives.

So they quitted the camp under the cataract, where they had spent several very enjoyable days.

Swiftly they descended the stream for several miles. Then, according to agreement, they hauled in at the head of the rapids for a lit tle restand consultation before making the riffle.

Will had declared his intention of going down the shore and taking up his position about midway of the drop, so as to snap off the two descending bullboats as they came flying along in the midst of the churning water. Afterward he and Mr. Mabie would enter the last boat and make the plunge.

When he was ready, with his camera focused, he waved his arm as a signal. Immediately one of the boats started forth, containing Bluff and Reddy. When they got fully into the swirl the second craft appeared in sight.

Jerry sat in the bow of this, and Frank in the stern, the more responsible position. Immediately the two adventurous cruisers were in the rapids, and shooting down with incredible swiftness.

The leading boat managed to pull through all right, for Reddy knew the route; but disaster awaited that containing the two chums. Whether they struck a half-submerged rock, and were capsized, or made a miscalculation, and found themselves seized by the cross-current, no one ever knew.

"Look out!" shouted Jerry, and the next instant both he and

Frank were overboard, and trying to keep away from the threatening snags while they went whirling down the rapids.

CHAPTER XVI

THE NEW CAMP

"Well, how did you like it, Jerry?"

"Talk to me about your shooting the whirlpool at Niagara in a barrel! That was bad enough for me! I swallowed enough water to float a ship! And here we are yet, each perched on a measly old slippery rock, in the middle of the rapids. Say! tell me about that, will you, Frank? How are we going to get ashore?"

The situation was comical as well as tragical. Just as Jerry said, each of the late inmates of the overturned bullboat, after being buffeted about furiously for several minutes, had succeeded in wildly scrambling on to an exposed rock.

There in midstream they sat, dripping wet, and with the foaming water surrounding them on all sides. In spite of his recent scare, Frank could not help laughing.

"What ails you? Perhaps you think I look funny?" exclaimed Jerry, who had received a few bruises, and was not feeling quite as cheerful as usual.

"Well, if you could only see yourself just now, you couldn't help laughing. Do you know you just put me in mind of that little god of good luck, Billikin!" called Frank, and in spite of his soreness Jerry had to grin in sympathy.

"Well, all right, then; there are two of us, and I guess you look as silly as I do. But there's that fellow, Will, getting his work in, as usual. A nice pair of geese we'll look like in his book of martyrs."

"Oh, that doesn't bother me one little bit just now. All I'm thinking about is how under the sun we're going to get out of this pickle," said Frank, sweeping his hand around, as if to call attention to the angry water that leaped and boiled in a frenzy of eagerness to get at its expected victims.

"Can't swim to the shore, that's sure. I suppose we'll just have to slip in again and make another turn of it. Thank goodness! the bottom of the old rapids is in sight, and as Bluff and Reddy have picked up our boat and the paddle, they could turn their hands at life saving when we came bobbing along."

"Hold on! Don't be rash, Jerry!" called Frank.

"Well, have you got anything better to say about it - any bright scheme to propose that offers to soften the blow?" demanded the other, pausing in his movement toward slipping off his unstable seat.

"I've just thought of something," answered Frank.

"Good for you, then. I guess I'm too badly rattled just now, for once, to do much thinking. What's the game, Frank?"

"Why not let Reddy and his reliable old rope come into play again?"

"Say! we'll have to beg or buy that clothesline from Reddy when we go away from here, and hang it up in our clubroom, as the most valuable asset we have. Without it what would become of us, eh? Talk about your trained nurses! That fellow is a whole hospital to the tenderfoot crowd. Call to him, please, and enlist his sympathy in the noble cause of yanking us in out of the wet."

So Frank did shout to the cowboy, who, having beached the two boats below the rapids, was hurrying up the shore. Mr. Mabie, too, had joined Will, so that presently the entire balance of the little party had gathered opposite.

Reddy entered into the game with spirit. He seemed to believe that these tragic occurrences must have just happened to give him a chance to show his skill in launching his rope.

"Jerry first, please!" called Frank.

"And why? Is it because I'm more valuable, or better-looking?" demanded Jerry.

"Oh, perhaps I want the pleasure of seeing how you look as you flounder through the rapids; and then, again, I may pick up a few points as to how *not* to do it."

"Tell me about that, will you! Some people have all the nerve!" shouted Jerry, for the rushing water made so much noise that an ordinary call could not have been heard.

Nevertheless, he accepted the flying noose that came shooting straight toward him, placed it under his arms, made sure that his gun was still fast to his back, and then fearlessly dropped off his perch.

There was considerable floundering on the part of the swimmer, much straining among the others who manipulated the rope, after which Jerry was assisted up the bank. His first act, after coughing up a lot of water, was to shake his fist at the grinning Frank, and then call out:

"Now you come on, and see how you like it!"

Frank did not wait upon the order of his going. As soon as he had the rope secured under his arms he slipped down into the foamy water, and began to buffet the current like a water spaniel.

After an exciting experience he, too, was drawn ashore, really none the worse for his adventure.

"Shake hands, Frank. You did nobly. I might have laughed, only I didn't seem to have breath enough," said Jerry, but the look in his eyes told how he had enjoyed seeing his chum passing through the same experience.

A fire was made, so that the soaked ones might dry off. Meanwhile, Mr. Mabie and Will succeeded in successfully shooting the rapids, though the latter was wise enough to leave his precious camera in the care of Bluff.

As noon found them still there, they took a "snack" before resuming the water journey. Below the fierce rapids the current was still swift, but there were places where the stream widened, and here the scenery was very fine, although the leaves looked more or less parched on account of the scarcity of rain during the summer that was passing.

An hour later, and they saw signs of smoke below.

"The boys have arrived ahead of us," said Mr. Mabie, pointing to the wreaths that ascended above the trees.

"All on account of our mishap. We lost three hours that way," remarked Frank, who felt a little provoked over the accident, since he aspired to be a capable canoeman at all times.

"Those things will happen to the best of guides at times," consoled the stockman. "I've often been in the drink myself. There are some cross-currents in our rapids, that one can only learn by experience. I rather expected you would go over, and instructed Reddy to be on the watch below."

"I wager I wouldn't get caught in that same way again, sir," asserted Frank.

"And I'm sure you wouldn't, lad. Experience is the best

teacher, and if we didn't have some of these bad turns we'd grow too confident."

The camp was soon looking quite cozy again, when the tents had been placed and everything made snug.

"I'm going to like this place almost as well as the one under the cascade," remarked Will, who had been rather skeptical all along.

So the first evening came along, and supper was the same hearty, enjoyable meal they had always found it. The camp appetites worked overtime, the coffee tasted splendid, the elk steaks were just what each one had been hungering for, and as the cook supplemented these with a heaping platter of flapjacks the contentment of the four chums seemed complete.

"How long do we stay here, Mr. Mabie?" asked Bluff, never hesitating when in search of information.

"Possibly a week or so. Then back to the ranch, and a new line of experiences. This terribly dry weather is making me anxious, for the range is drying up, and we shall be hard set to find pasture for the cattle soon, unless rain comes along."

"Do you have such a dry spell in summer often up here?" asked Frank.

"Never saw the equal of this since I settled in the valley, many years ago. Now, down in Ohio, where I originally came from, they have drouths even in May, at times, and I've seen things go to the dogs more than once, gardens dried up, and even a forest fire in July, but never up here," replied the stockman.

"The woods look as though it wouldn't take a great deal to set them going," declared Frank. "One of the men threw a match down to-day, after lighting his cigarette, and it seemed like magic the way the fire flashed up. He had to be quick to jump on it before the breeze carried it along."

Mr. Mabie frowned.

"I won't ask you which man it was, Frank; but I must warn them again to be more than ordinarily careful about throwing matches around and leaving a fire burning anywhere in the woods. Many a grand forest has been ruined by such carelessness," he said.

"How does that happen, sir?" inquired Bluff.

"It is easy. The careless hunter or trapper leaves his dying fire when he breaks camp. Then up comes a sudden wind and some of the red cinders are blown into the dead leaves or punk grass. Fanned by the breeze, they become a roaring flame in a minute, and the mischief is done. Be careful, boys, please."

"We certainly will, sir," replied Frank sincerely. "Not to speak of the damage done, it must be mighty unpleasant to be caught in a forest fire. I've read of such things, but never hankered for a personal experience."

On the following day they started to look into the possibilities for big game around the new camp.

"Reddy, here, says he knows of a bear den that we ought to visit some time later. While at it, you boys must see all there is going in the way of sport, for you may never come out this way again, though I hope that will not be the case. To-day, however, we will take things a bit easy," remarked the ranchman.

Although the stockman did not speak any plainer, Frank knew just what he meant.

"He thinks we must be feeling the effects of our little excitement yesterday, Jerry, and that the soreness in our muscles will take our ambition away for to-day," he said aside to his chum.

"Tell me about that, will you! To prove that we're tougher than Mr. Mabie thinks, let's you and I engineer a little hunt of our own?" proposed the other quickly.

Accordingly, they started out, going down the valley.

"The walk will do us good, anyhow," declared Frank, "even if we don't run across any big game."

"I was asking Mr. Mabie about moose, and he said that occasionally one is seen in this region, though generally they hang out further east. I've always wanted to get a moose, but was never able to be up in the woods where they are found, when the law was off. How about you, Frank? Ever shoot at one?"

"Never had that luck, though I've seen many in the summer time, in Maine. Somehow, it seems to go against the grain doing this hunting at such a queer time. I guess it won't be long before they have as strict laws up here as we have to protect such game as deer and elk."

"How about panthers and grizzlies?" asked Jerry.

"They don't want to protect those fellows. You've got a right to knock one over, or a wolf, any time you want, if he doesn't get you first," laughed Frank.

An hour later they separated, Frank to look along one ridge, while Jerry had taken a notion to see what the other might have in the shape of game.

Frank spent quite a long time scouring the woods that covered the side of the valley. He had not put up anything worth while, and was even thinking about heading back to the place where he had agreed to meet his chum, when a distressing little accident occurred.

Just as he was hurrying down a steep bank his foot caught in a vine, and he was hurled forward with such violence that his head, coming in contact with the hard ground, received such a blow that he was rendered unconscious.

Frank never knew just how long he remained insensible. It might have been only a few minutes, or perhaps half an hour slipped by while he lay there. When he finally opened his eyes he looked up into a dusky face, and realized that it belonged to an Indian!

CHAPTER XVII

AT THE CAMPFIRE OF THE CREES

Frank was not at all alarmed. In the first place, he had been assured by Mr. Mabie that these Crees were not inclined to be hostile. Then, again, he saw that it was no fierce face of a warrior that bent over him, but the pitying one of a child.

"Hello! Who are you?" he asked, a little weakly, for his head was still swimming more or less from his shock.

"Little Mink," came the reply, though the boy apparently had to nerve himself to keep from running away.

"And you found me knocked out, did you? What are you doing here, Little Mink?" Frank sat up as he spoke, though he realized that he would be unsteady on his feet when he tried to stand.

"Teepee down by river, not far off. Little Mink have snare for rabbit. Him go see if ketch one, find paleface here. Think dead, then him open eyes. Good!"

Frank was amused at the air of the little fellow. He knew something about the ways of civilized Indians, having been among them in Maine, hence he could see that this boy was endeavoring to ape the manners of his elders.

"Would you help me get down to your camp, Little Mink? I

feel weak after my tumble, and my own camp is far away," he said.

Now, Frank knew very well that a loud shout would, in all probability, have fetched Jerry to the spot. He had an object in making this appeal to the Indian lad, and watched his dusky face closely as the other considered the proposal.

Perhaps Frank, fearing a refusal, may have put on more agony than the state of his feelings really warranted. At any rate, he succeeded in swerving the boy from a condition of caution to that of sympathy.

"Little Mink help. Him lead paleface to teepee," he said, and the look that accompanied the words told Frank as plainly as words could have done that the boy was trusting in his honor not to betray them.

Accordingly, he hung on to the lad, and in this fashion they went for half a mile or so, when the river was reached. Presently Frank discovered signs of a camp not far in the distance. A little pale smoke was rising over the thicket, and he also saw a conical skin teepee, while on the shore were three bullboats.

As Little Mink came into camp, assisting the white hunter, several squaws began an excited jabber that brought out a couple of bucks.

"A hungry-looking lot all around," was the mental comment of the young hunter.

He had seen that Little Mink did not look as though he had enjoyed a bountiful share of food lately, and the rest of the party were certainly no better off.

One of the bucks was an old man, yet he seemed to have a certain dignity about him. Frank's curiosity was now greater than ever. He made up his mind that there was something singular about this party of Crees who seemed to be wandering in the wilderness without guns, or any means for obtaining food, and, if possible, he meant to discover what the secret could be.

The old Indian approached, looking suspiciously at him. Frank put out his hand at once in a cordial manner.

"How!" he said, smiling in his engaging manner.

The other at once fell under the charm of Frank's smile.

"White boy much hurt?" he asked, looking at the dirt and blood on Frank's left hand, where he had cut himself slightly.

"No. I had a bad fall, and feel weak. Little Mink found me lying there, and let me come with him to your camp. I have friends above, a hunting party under the charge of Mr. Mabie, the stockman."

He saw the old fellow move uneasily at mention of the name.

"Shoot elk?" asked the other, nodding.

"Yes, sometimes, with gun," and Frank purposely held up his repeating rifle.

He saw the black eyes glitter enviously at sight of it, which made his curiosity only the stronger.

"Bad! bad!" muttered the Indian, though he did not explain what he meant; but Frank believed he must be thinking of the theft of the elk some days previous.

"You no guns here?" he asked, and the old Indian shook his head sadly, though a look of sudden anger also flitted across his strong face.

"Nothing, only hatchet and one knife. Take all else away when send us out from village. No care if squaw and pappoose die from hunger. Bad! bad! But some day p'raps Running Elk go back and make change. Wait! wait! No sleep on trail!"

Already was Frank beginning to see behind the mystery. For some cause this old brave and his immediate family had been chased out of the Cree village, many miles to the northwest. Deprived of weapons, they had been started on the river in the bullboats, to meet what fate had in store for them.

No wonder, then, that coming unexpectedly on the dead elk Bluff had shot, they had stolen it, for hunger stalked in their miserable camp, and the pappooses cried for the food the braves could not supply.

The only thing that still puzzled Frank was why they had not appealed to some of the whites. But there must be some good reason, he argued, for this. Perhaps it was only the natural pride an Indian feels, and which prevents him from admitting to the palefaces that he is helpless to supply the wants of his people.

"Name Frank," he said, touching his breast "What call you?"

"Running Elk, chief among Crees. Long he lead them in the hunt and in battle. But a serpent come among my people and poison all against Running Elk. Now they think the half-breed Pierre La Motte best man to follow. Him talk, talk, all time, and warriors dream. Some day they wake up and know him for bad man. Then p'raps they ask Running Elk come back again. Wait, see!"

That was the Indian idea of patience. Frank could understand it all now. Plainly, a smart half-breed had managed to hypnotize the braves in the Cree village, and influence them to turn against their own chief. When he and his family resisted they were ignominiously exiled, and sent forth to face the world without means for providing food for the squaws and pappooses.

Somehow, Frank felt a strong sense of sympathy for the old exiled chief.

"You see the rancher, Mr. Mabie. I think he can do something for you," he said.

"I know him. He no like Running Elk and the Crees. Once they take some cattle that stampede and wander far away. Never forget or forgive that wrong. Better not see rancher. Go on down river soon, sell few pelts, and buy gun. Mebbe all right."

"No! no! Don't be in a hurry. I'm sure Mr. Mabie won't hold that old grudge against you now, and he's a good man. He will give you gun and powder. Wait and see."

Half an hour later, as he was sitting there, with a rude bandage around his throbbing head, and talking with Little Mink, who had taken a great fancy for the paleface hunter who owned the beautiful gun, Frank heard a startled exclamation from the border of the thicket near by.

"Hello, there, Jerry! Come in and get acquainted!" he cried out, as his eyes fell upon the astonished face of his chum thrust from the scrub.

"Talk to me about surprises! What could equal this? Here, after getting the scare of my life, thinking my chum had been carried off by the redskins, I find him hobnobbing with them in their camp. Sure they ain't dangerous, Frank?" asked Jerry, advancing cautiously, with his gun held ready.

"As mild as an old lady's cup of tea. Wouldn't hurt a fly. Sit down, and I'll tell you all about them," said Frank.

"First, I want to know are you hurt much? I happened on where you fell, and just imagine my alarm when I saw the print of little moccasins. Why, I was sure some frisky red had knocked you over the head with a warclub, and then toted you off to be burned at the stake. I followed as well as I could, bent on rescuing you at the peril of my life, to meet up with a reception like this."

Frank was compelled to laugh at the look of evident disgust that came over the countenance of his comrade.

But when Jerry had heard all his chum knew concerning the little band of wandering Crees, his generous heart was stirred at the thought of their wrongs.

"That greedy half-breed ought to be made to walk the plank, that's what! Just to think of the nerve of him chasing the genuine dyed-in-the-wool chief out into the cold and taking his place! Why, he's a usurper, that's the truth! And look here, Frank, didn't you hear what Mr. Mabie said about a fellow named Pierre La Motte?"

"I must have been away at the time. What did he say?" asked Frank eagerly.

"Why, there was a detachment of the sheriff's posse at the ranch house just before we came, looking for that same fellow. Seems that he's wanted badly for something or other."

"Hurrah! That's just what I was hoping would happen. We can put them wise about Pierre, and they'll go after him. Then, perhaps, as old Running Elk says, when the man with the smooth tongue has gone away forever, the Crees will send and beg their chief to return, and forgive the past. It's all right! I'll bring him here to see you."

But Running Elk had already learned that another stranger was in camp, and even then he was approaching, looking considerably embarrassed, for he feared it might be Mr. Mabie himself.

However, he was soon set at his ease. What Frank had to say about the bad half-breed also gave him new pleasure.

"Not wait long now," he said, nodding his head sagely, while his beady eyes fairly glittered with satisfaction, as in imagination he saw his hated foe being taken away from the Cree village by the much-feared sheriff's posse.

CHAPTER XVIII

AN INVITATION TO COME OUT

"About time those boys were showing up, eh, Bluff?"

"There they come now, Mr. Mabie, and - Jerusalem!"

"What ails you now?" asked the stockman, coming out of the tent.

"They've got an old Indian in tow, as sure as you live!" cried Bluff.

"Where is he? I've just been wanting to get an Indian picture the worst way. Show him to me, please!" And Will came crawling hastily forth, of course clutching his beloved camera in his hand.

"H'm! I guess I know that old buck. It's Running Elk, the chief of the Crees. Something must have happened out of the usual order," said the ranchman.

When he learned what Frank had to say Mr. Mabie proved himself just such a man as the others had believed him to be. He advanced to the Indian, who was standing there in stoical silence, with his blanket thrown over his shoulder, and held out his hand.

"I'm glad to meet you again, Running Elk, and sorry to hear

about your trouble. But it will soon be all right. I'll see to it that the authorities learn about Pierre, and they'll get him before long. In the meantime, I'm going to give you a letter to my foreman. You take your little party to the ranch, and they'll see to it that you have plenty to eat until I come back home," he said.

The chief shook his head sadly.

"Bad! bad! Young braves no think when kill runaway steers. Never more can happen after this. Send skins to pay when get um. Glad get meat for squaw and pappoose."

That was the extent of his remarks.

"I guess Injuns ain't got much of a supply of words," remarked Will aside to Bluff.

"But he means all right. I like the old chap's looks. Come along, Frank, and tell us all about it. You look like you've been in a fight. Say! The reds didn't tackle you, did they?" exclaimed Bluff.

"One did; a little chap about hip-high. Ho was out trying to snare a jack-rabbit, when he found me. I'd taken a header down over a root, and was lying in a state where I didn't care whether school kept or not. He led me to their camp, and Jerry found me there later. That's all of it in a nutshell. Now I'm going to have Mr. Mabie wrap up my hand and take a look at my head, for it still rings."

After an examination, the ranchman declared that there was nothing serious the matter.

"It may take a few days for that lump to subside, and these cuts to heal, but you came out of it better than an old fellow like me could have done," he said, and Frank felt relieved.

"What are you going to do with Running Elk?" he asked.

"Send him back to his people with some food. Then he will carry this letter to my foreman, who will look after the party until we get back. After that I'll see to it that Pierre is taken care of and the chief recalled to his own."

"I knew you would. I told the old fellow that, but he was sore afraid that you could never forgive what his young braves had done a year or two ago."

The old Cree chief soon departed, with a grin on his face, and his arms full of bundles. He might have been proud, but there were hungry mouths to feed, and for their sakes he must forget that he should die sooner than beg favors.

Frank felt rather stiff and sore on the following day. He was satisfied to hang about camp, and let his chums do the hunting, for once.

Jerry could not be restrained, for his sporting blood demanded that he keep going all the while. Will was just as eager to do his style of shooting, and even wandered down the river to get a view of the Cree teepee before the family of Running Elk broke camp.

Bluff took a notion to try fishing, and with considerable success. Later in the day Frank also wet a line, and between them they managed to secure a decent mess of fat trout for the whole party.

When Jerry came in he reported that he had had a shot at an elk, but failed to stop his flight. He also declared that he had seen what he believed to be a wolf skulking through the timber.

"Oh, I don't doubt it," said the old stockman, when Frank looked questioningly at him. "The pesky critters like to hang around here, looking for a nice calf that happens to stray away from its mammy's side. Winter and summer, it's all the same to them, so long as we don't get after the pack too hot. Never lose a chance to knock over a wolf, my boy."

"I never mean to," said Jerry, holding up a piece of gray fur.

"That's wolf, all right; and look here, what did you do to him?" demanded Mr. Mabie.

"I was very kind to the scamp, and hung him up in a tree, where the rest of his tribe couldn't get at him to tear his hide to pieces. You see, I had a notion that I'd like to have that skin for a rug, and that later on, perhaps, one of the boys might go out with me and remove it much better than I could," grinned Jerry.

"Thank you, my lad. I feel that you've done me a favor. Every wolf that goes across the Great Divide means more calves to grow up; and you shall have your rug, I pledge you my word."

Mr. Mabie shook the hand of the successful wolf hunter with emphasis, showing that he felt deeply on the subject.

Just as he expected, Frank was still rather sore on the following day. He let the others do the hunting that morning, Will tagging behind the bunch with his ready camera.

They came in at noon, having covered some new ground, and brought the best part of an elk with them. Mr. Mabie laughed, and wished it might have been an antelope instead. He was not partial to elk meat, which was perhaps natural in a stockman, who could kill young beef whenever the spirit moved.

"How about that bear den, Reddy?" asked Jerry, as they lounged about the camp in the early afternoon.

"Any time you say the word. I was only waitin' till Frank felt himself again," was the other's reply.

"Oh, don't let my condition keep you from that little entertainment. Besides, I feel much better now. Perhaps a little excitement might put me in just the right kind of trim," declared that individual promptly.

"Hear! hear!" exclaimed Bluff, making a pretense of clapping his hands.

"Talk to me about your dyed-in-the-wool sportsman! Frank, here, could give any fellow points," declared Jerry.

"I understand the principle he works on. It's the same as what they call homoepathy, that 'like cures like.' I've seen a man, when struck by a rattler, chase the reptile, kill him, and apply his crushed body to the wound, in the belief that one poison would counteract the other," said the stockman.

"Did it succeed?" asked Jerry, eager for information along these lines.

"Well," said Mr. Mabie, "the poor chap died, I'm sorry to say. In another case, the fellow insisted on filling himself up with whiskey. He lived through it, too, which proved the rule, though I believe there are better things to save a man than liquor. But Frank has the right idea. The excitement of the chase will cause him to forget, and take some of the stiffness out of his joints."

"Then we go this afternoon?" queried Reddy anxiously.

"Whenever you're ready," answered Frank.

They set out within half an hour. Of course, the whole four chumsinsisted on being in the party. Besides, there were the guide, Mr. Mabie and Billy. Each of the cowboys carried his rope, for of late it had seemed as though a lariat might be a very necessary accompaniment to these side hunts.

They headed in a quarter where, as yet, none of the boys had been. This led them directly into the thickets that lay at the base of the mountain barrier, stretching away up against the blue heavens.

None of the chums had forgotten the fierce appearance of the grizzly that had fallen before the rifle which Jerry wielded so cleverly.

"Remember, lads," said Mr. Mabie, as they trailed along through rocky gulches, "every Mountain Charlie isn't going to keel over as easily as the one Jerry got. He was lucky to send his lead to a vital point. I've seen veteran hunters shoot a bear a dozen times, and then have to finish him with a knife."

"I've always read that they can stand a tremendous amount of shooting without caving under," admitted Frank.

"And it isn't considered at all disgraceful, when stirring such a terrible monster out of his den, for the hunters to post themselves in trees near by. While at first blush such a procedure might seem silly or cowardly to you, take an old hunter's advice, and give the rascal no more chance than you can help. Even then I've known him to shake a fellow out of a small tree, and only for the assistance of the others he must have killed the youngster."

"A grizzly can't climb a tree, then, sir?" questioned Will uneasily.

"Not ordinarily. He might manage to swarm up if the trunk was inclined about forty-five degrees. Select straight ones, and of some size; then you're safe."

"Thank you, Mr. Mabie. I'll follow your advice. You see, I'm only the photographer of the club, and they could hardly afford to lose me," remarked Will, thinking some sort of an apology might be necessary for his seeming timidity.

But the others did not laugh. They knew their chum too well for that. He had proven more than once that when it came to a pinch he could conquer his natural weakness, and show the right spirit of bravery, especially if it were one of his comrades who was in peril.

"Well," remarked Reddy a short time later, "we're close to the place now."

"I imagined as much," said Mr. Mabie, with a significant look around.

"You mean that this is an ideal spot for a grizzly to have his den?" asked Jerry.

"Fine. Look at the tumbled-down rocks, making many a cave that affords shelter from the elements, winter and summer. Then, of course, the old rascal has a nice short cut through some canyon to the open country. He uses that when he feels sharp set for veal. Oh, yes, I've no doubt he's been the cause of many a calf disappearing from the herd," said the stockman between his teeth.

"I don't wonder, then, you are so keen at wanting to get rid of all such neighbors as grizzlies, panthers and wolves. They make an expensive boarding-house," laughed Bluff.

"They take their toll right along. This region would be a paradise for a stockman only for that. The grass is heavy, and while the winters are severe, we know how to carry our stock over; but we can never calculate our profits, because of the losses on account of hungry wild beasts."

"Then I'm glad we came here to get our taste of big-game shooting, for it will not only be fun for us, but a benefit to civilization," remarked Bluff, who, being in training to succeed his lawyer father, often liked to indulge in imposing sentences.

"Now look over yonder to where that cleft yawns," said Reddy at this juncture.

"I see it; and is that the den?" asked Jerry.

"Sure as you live. You fellows be choosing your trees, and let me take a peek."

"He isn't going in, I hope!" exclaimed Will as the cowboy moved away.

"Well, hardly. Reddy doesn't want to commit suicide just yet. He's only going to make sure the old chap is at home, then he'll make preparations to smoke him out."

As Mr. Mabie said, Reddy was soon back, and from his actions it was positive the bear was at home. He began collecting dry wood and all manner of material calculated to make a big smoke. The boys knew something about such a scheme themselves, and were deeply interested.

Mr. Mabie insisted that each one seek an asylum in the branches of a tree that commanded the black cleft. Presently, Reddy had his pile of wood and brush ready, and he put a match to it, after which he beat a hasty retreat, climbing into the tree with Frank.

"Listen!" he said presently.

Frank could hear a sound like sneezing. This was followed by a scrambling noise that arose above the crackling of the fire. Then came a terrific roar, succeeded by a sudden scattering of the brands, and the enraged grizzly rushed into the open!

CHAPTER XIX

A STRANGE DISCLOSURE

"Hello, there, Charlie! How's your health?"

Reddy swung himself down from the limb on which he had been perched, and kicked out with his feet in such a way that he attracted the attention of the beast.

"He's coming! Look out, Frank!" shouted Will, who, secure in his perch, had, of course, been manipulating his camera with burning zeal.

Bang!

It was Bluff who had fired, but if he hit the great beast at all, the latter minded the wound no more than he would a flea bite.

Jerry also took a turn as the grizzly passed the tree in which he was hidden.

"I hit him!" he whooped as the grizzly gave a snap backward at his flank.

But the enticement offered by Reddy's swinging form proved too much for the enraged animal. Doubtless he imagined that all his troubles came from that biped or monkey hanging up yonder, just within reach of his claws if he arose on his hind legs. Hence his eagerness to make the attempt.

"Pull up, quick!" exclaimed Frank as the grizzly rushed under the tree and immediately started to rear up.

The daring cowboy had held out until the very last second, meaning that nothing should balk his design of enticing the enemy under their refuge, where Frank could get in his work.

Afterward Frank understood his motive. Reddy was especially fond of him, though he also liked all of the other chums. He believed that Jerry had secured enough honors in being given the chance to knock over the other bear, and it was his desire to see Frank even up the score.

Just in the nick of time the cowboy swung his legs up around the limb. The horrible claws of the grizzly swept through the air not a foot below where he had hung. Frank shuddered at the consequences had anything happened to bring Reddy within reach of such a powerful beast.

"Now get him, Frank!" gasped the one who hung on with arms and legs.

Neither Bluff nor Jerry thought to shoot a second time. They seemed to understand that the game had passed them by, and that it was Frank's turn.

When he saw the right chance the young sportsman pulled the trigger. He had not made any mistake in judging just where he should aim, for with the report of his rifle the grizzly floundered, and fell over.

"Wow! That did the business!" shouted Jerry.

"Hold on, boys! Don't get down yet!" called Mr. Mabie hastily, as he thought he detected a disposition on the part of either Bluff or Jerry to drop from their secure perches to the ground.

It was well they refrained, for already the monster was once more on his feet, and, roaring with fury, endeavoring to reach the enemies who clung there so tantalizingly, just beyond his extended claws.

"Give him another!" cried Reddy promptly.

Frank did; and wishing to end the beast as quickly as possible, he aimed to send the lead straight to the heart. But he was compelled to use every bullet in his six-shot repeater before the giant received his quietus, and rolled over, to rise no more.

Frank had a queer feeling as he dropped to the ground and stood over his big game. Deep down in his heart he envied his chum, because Jerry had been able to kill *his* grizzly while the beast was charging him.

"It may be all right," he said to Mr. Mabie, "and it's a good thing to get rid of these savage animals in any old way, but I hope I don't take part in another affair like this. He had no chance, poor old chap."

The old rancher looked admiringly at the boy.

"Those sentiments do you proud, lad, and I appreciate them, too; but business, in my line, must go ahead of sentiment, and this old Charlie was doing me a bad turn. My herds will rest easier now that he is gone," he said feelingly.

Leaving Billy and Reddy to secure the hide of the second grizzly, the others returned to camp. Restless Jerry tried the fishing again, and as before, success came his way.

"I'd give something to have my little *Red Rover* here, in that swift water," sighed Bluff, as he and Frank sat on the edge of the bluff, listening to the rush of the river while it sped on its way to the lower country.

"Well, a canoe might be fine for shooting downstream, but I

don't believe you'd find it as safe in the rapids as those hide boats. The rocks can't smash in their sides, like cedar or canvas craft. Better to do as the natives do, I find, whenever I go anywhere. They know by experience what's best," returned Frank wisely.

"Look there! A cowboy coming like the wind up the river, waving his hat over his head! Say! d'ye suppose anything's gone wrong at the ranch, and we'll have to cut our hunt short?" exclaimed Bluff anxiously.

"Oh, I guess not. You see, those fellows are built that way. They never can do anything without excitement. See! He's holding up something that looks like a mail pouch," said Frank composedly.

"Why, of course that's it! I heard Mr. Mabie say he expected mail to-day, and, for one, I'll be mighty glad to hear from the folks," sighed Bluff.

"What? Not getting homesick already, I hope?" smiled his chum.

"Certainly not, only a fellow naturally likes to hear from his mom and dad when he's away so far," declared Bluff stoutly.

"Yes, and also from some other fellow's sister, in the bargain. Nellie never finds time to write to me when I'm away, leaving all that to the old folks; but I notice that you always manage to get a letter in her handwriting."

"Well, I made her solemnly promise to write every other day, you see," explained Bluff, while he suddenly became red in the face, hurrying off to get his mail.

There were letters for all the boys. Jerry was called in from his entrancing sport to receive his share, and Frank noticed that he, too, had a sweet-looking missive in a schoolgirl hand. Of course, it must be from Mame Crosby, for Jerry and she were great friends.

"Here's something enclosed in my letter, and directed to Mr. Frank Langdon. Does anybody know a fellow by that name?" asked Will, holding up a delicate envelope that seemed to exhale a fragrance all its own.

"And sealed, too! What a breach of etiquette!" jeered Jerry.

"Now, *will* you be good?" observed Bluff, glad of a chance to return the favor.

"That's all right. Possibly Violet wants to make some inquiries concerning her twin brother, how he behaves, and if he has developed any rash spirit calculated to get him into trouble. I remember telling her that if she felt anxious just to drop me a line, and I'd answer."

Frank unblushingly took the envelope from the extended fingers of Will.

"Open it!" commanded Bluff.

"You'll have to excuse me, fellows. That wouldn't be hardly fair to my correspondent, you know. She expects me to keep her secrets." And Frank coolly sauntered off as he spoke.

Nor did he ever take them into his confidence with regard to what the contents of that scented missive might be. Even Will was not told. However, like most brothers, it can be said that he did not seem overly anxious to learn. He had, perhaps, secrets of his own.

Once again they were seated around the campfire. Supper had been, as usual, a great success, and while the older members of the party smoked, our boys amused themselves in various ways.

Will was, of course, busy with his photographic outfit. His

field dark-room was a success, and he developed his films, and did all other things necessary, with little or no trouble. Indeed, he had an apparatus whereby he could carry on this operation successfully even in the daytime; but he usually worked at night, because there was nothing else going on then.

The others had fallen into a conversation connected with their home life. Reddy hovered near, listening, and Frank wondered why that wistful look had come into the eyes of the young cowboy. Possibly he had a home somewhere - perhaps memories of a mother or father had crowded into his mind while the boys were talking of the sacred ties that bound them to Centerville.

Frank had always believed there must be something of a history attached to Reddy's past. He had even hoped that some time the other might take such a liking to him as to speak of his own folks. His manner gave Frank the impression that the dashing cowboy might have had a new longing spring up in his breast since their coming to the ranch, a desire to once again visit the scenes of his boyhood.

So, as they talked, referring to many of the events of the past, names were often mentioned, and as a thought came to him, Frank happened to say:

"I wonder how Hank Brady is getting on with father's new car?"

He saw the cowboy start and turn white.

"Who's Hank Brady?" he asked, his voice trembling.

"A fellow we met under strange circumstances. Hank was on the road to the bad, but he got his eyes open just in time. Now he's our chauffeur, and we think he's going to make good," replied Frank, watching the other with sudden interest.

"Huh! Did you ever hear anything about his family?" asked

Reddy, trying to act in a natural manner, but hardly succeeding very well.

"Yes. He's got a father and mother who were mighty anxious about him."

"And there's that good-for-nothing brother Ted he told you to keep your eye out for up here!" broke in Bluff.

"Yes; how about that, Frank? Have you ever asked about him?" exclaimed Jerry.

"No; but perhaps I'd better begin now. How about it, Reddy?" questioned Frank.

"You needn't go any further, for I can tell you all about that scalawag. If you had asked Mr. Mabie, he'd have told you my name was Ted Brady," was the astonishing reply.

CHAPTER XX

"WE MUST CUT AND RUN FOR IT!"

It was surprising to see the effect of the cowboy's announcement.

Frank was in some measure prepared for it. He had entertained a sudden suspicion as he noticed the emotion of the other. But his chums seemed almost thunderstruck.

"Tell me about that, will you!" said Jerry, feebly waving his hands.

"Did you ever hear of such luck?" ejaculated Will.

"Beats a story all hollow. Here's the prodigal son found at last, eating his dinner with the -" began Bluff, when Jerry pounced on him.

"Don't you dare finish that, on your life! Of course, you can call yourself swine, if you please, but I object. But is it really true, Reddy? Are you Hank's long lost brother?" he asked, turning to the other.

"I certainly am, although I ought to be ashamed of the way I've treated my folks. All for a measly little matter, too. My eyes have been openin' lately, and I was mighty near headin' Eastways before you came," said the cowboy, hanging his head.

"Then perhaps you'll go back with us, and surprise the folks?" suggested Frank eagerly.

"Well, now, I'd like to do that same, if so be you fellows mean it. You see, my folks ain't always lived in Centerville. I thought that lots of things you talked about seemed kinder familiar to me, for I was brought up in that part of the State. Yes, I'll go home, and try and make up for what I done to hurt the old folks. Somehow, just the idea of it makes me feel better."

He eagerly questioned the boys about his people. Of course, they did not have much news to tell him. Hank was only a year or so older than his brother, and the absent one was very much interested in hearing how they had met him, and what awakened Hank to a consciousness of the terrible mistake he was making in associating with unscrupulous men.

After that Reddy assumed a new place with the boys. He seemed to be closer to them than ever, and Frank no longer wondered why the other's sunburned face had seemed partly familiar to him when he first met him.

"You and Hank are very much alike," he said, later on, to Reddy.

"They used to say that at home. I was just big enough to be accused of many of Hank's tricks, and once I got a lickin' he deserved."

"And another thing," laughed Frank, "I know now what he was about to tell me at the time I was dragged away by my folks. I was asking him how I could ever recognize you, in case we met, and he put up his hand to his head, but I never heard the rest of it."

"Why, of course, he was going to tell you that I had a mop of beautiful red hair, and that Teddy went with Reddy. I guess you'd have known me if you'd heard that," was the good-natured remark of the found one.

On the following day the four outdoor chums determined to set out in a bunch to have a grand hunt, following the dense woods far down the valley. The last words of the old stockman were a caution in connection with the dry grass.

"Be careful about a fire, lads. If you make one, be sure the last spark is out before you leave it. A forest fire would play the mischief just now, with everything so dry. But somehow, I've got hopes that the rain is coming soon," and he looked into the west, as though the few low-down clouds gave him encouragement.

When noon came the boys had put up a couple of elk, but at such a distance that no one but Bluff fired, and he because he knew no better.

"Do you think I wounded him?" he had the nerve to ask, whereat Jerry looked at Frank and just smiled broadly.

"Anyhow, they ran off faster after I fired," asserted Bluff confidently.

"I should think anything would," was all Jerry said, and if there was malice in the remark Bluff did not know it in his innocence.

While they sat down to eat the lunch they had carried along Frank called attention to the fact that the wind had risen.

"Perhaps Mr. Mabie was right, after all, and there is a rainstorm coming before long," suggested Will.

"Then I hope it'll have the decency to hold off until we get home," said Bluff.

"Oh, a little wetting wouldn't hurt us. We're not made of sugar or salt. But perhaps we'd better not go any further. We've come a long way since breakfast. This valley seems to have no end, and it broadens out down here, too."

"Yes; and, Frank, have you noticed how thick the trees grow, too? Why, in some places a fat man would have trouble getting through between the trunks," said Jerry.

"What ails Frank? He seems to be sniffing the air like a hound," asked Will.

"Oh, he always declared he had a fine scent, and I've noticed that he knows when dinner is ready, ahead of the rest of us," remarked Jerry.

Frank laughed good-naturedly.

"To tell the truth, I was wondering, fellows, whether we could be near another camp," he remarked.

"Did you hear anybody shout?" asked Will.

"No; but when there came a sudden shift to the wind I thought I got a scent of fire. No, it wasn't cooking, this time, Jerry, so don't get ready to accuse me of that weakness again; just something burning."

"Say! you don't think it could be the woods afire, do you?"

"Talk to me about your ghost-seers, will you! Will, here, can jump on to trouble quicker than any fellow I know. Why, if the woods were on fire, don't you think we'd have found that fact out before now, Mr. Faint Heart? I guess such a thing couldn't happen without a heap of smoke that would look like a pall, and appal us, in the bargain."

"Well, all I can say is, I'm not hankering after any forest fire experience after what Mr. Mabie told us about those friends of his who were nearly burned to death seven years ago; and that was a prairie fire, too," observed Will, continuing to cast anxious glances around.

"Amen to that," remarked Bluff.

"Why, you must think I'm just wild to try my legs, with a healthy blaze jumping after me; but I'm not, all the same. Come along, Lazy-bones! We're going to have the delightful pleasure of covering those ten miles back again," and Jerry pulled Will to his feet.

"Ten miles!" groaned the other dismally, making a pretense of hobbling, as if his muscles had given out. "How in the world can I ever do it?"

"Well, sing out when you want to stop. We'll hang you up in a tree, safe and sound, just as I did that wolf I got; and later on one of the boys can come for you with a horse," was Jerry's cheerful remark.

"Oh, I'd hate to put you to any additional trouble, so I'll try my best to limp along," replied Will, who, of course, was only shamming, in that he was not half so tired as he tried to make out.

So they turned their faces toward the home camp, and started trudging along, now and then calling to one another as something caught their fancy.

Will had had little opportunity to make use of his picture-taking machine this trip. His stock of films was beginning to run low, and only special subjects must claim his attention from now on. Besides, he had several views of the great woods, and the light was so poor under the trees that it required a time exposure to bring out the details.

"I think it's a mean shame none of you fellows think enough of me to get up some sort of excitement, in order to let me snap you off," he was saying as he tramped along.

"Tell me about that, will you! The chap really thinks that it's our duty to do all sorts of remarkable stunts, in order that he may have the pleasure of snapping us off in ridiculous positions!"

"Hear! hear! That was the finest speech I ever knew Jerry to put up. As a rule, he leaves the heavy talk to me, and is satisfied to just grunt out his ideas. But look here, Frank, I believe you were right," said Bluff, stopping to elevate his nose in a significant fashion.

"Oh! dear me! Do you smell smoke, too?" demanded Will.

"Why, so do I, now that you mention it. And say! just cast your eyes back of us, fellows! Don't it seem as though there was more or less smoke in the woods over yonder?" asked Jerry.

The four boys now showed sudden animation.

"Hark to the wind, too! It's beginning to make a sound up there in the tree-tops. Which way is it coming, Frank?" asked Will.

Frank's face began to assume a serious look. The wind was fairly growing stronger with every passing minute. If the woods should be afire, this would whip the flames furiously, and send them speeding along at a dangerous pace.

"It begins to look bad for us, boys," he remarked.

"What! Do you really mean it, or are you just trying to play a joke?"

"You know me better than that, Will. There is certainly a brush fire back there. Some camper has left his fire, and the rising wind has carried it into the dead leaves," said Frank soberly, surveying his surroundings.

"Could we push forward and put it out before it does any damage?" asked Bluff.

"I'm afraid it's too late for that now. See there! The smoke is getting thicker and thicker all the time. Boys, we might as well look the matter straight in the face."

"What do you mean, Frank?" asked Will in a trembling voice.

"We must cut and run for it, that's all, for the fire is coming swiftly!"

CHAPTER XXI

NEVER GIVE UP

At first, the boys made light of the flight. All of them were pretty fair runners, and although the weather was warm for such exertion, they did some clever work.

"It's getting worse back there!" said Will, who brought up the rear.

Frank had known this for several minutes, and was correspondingly worried.

The wind had risen to such an extent that it rushed through the tree-tops like an express train, making a doleful sound. Nor was this all, for they could plainly hear a crackling from the rear that was gradually becoming a subdued roar.

"Oh! I saw the fire then!" called Will a minute or two later.

Looking over their shoulders as they ran, all of them had glimpses of the flames leaping hungrily upward. What Mr. Mabie had feared all along had actually come to pass. All of them were glad, however, that it had not been through any fault of theirs, since they had built no fire that day.

"Frank, it's catching up with us! Whatever shall we do?" panted Bluff, close beside the one he addressed.

Frank had been considering this same question. He at first thought they might outrun the fire, but now he changed his mind. The woods were so dense, and the vegetation so thick, that whenever they tried to make fast time they kept tripping over trailing vines, or else banging up against the trunks of the forest monarchs, sometimes damaging their noses by the contact.

"What was he telling us about fighting fire with fire?" asked Jerry, who was by this time feeling not quite so jaunty as usual, but ready to seize upon any opening that promised safety.

"That was out on the prairie. I don't think the scheme would work here in the woods. It would take too long for the second blaze to get a start, and we'd be caught between the two fires," was Frank's reply.

"But we must do something pretty soon!" cried Will.

Indeed, it would appear so. They were now enveloped in a pall of smoke, that, entering their eyes, made them smart fiercely. Not only that, but the fire could be seen in a dozen places behind them, leaping up into the trees as the dried foliage offered such a splendid torch, and the wind urged the conflagration along.

"Will's right. The old thing's running us neck and crop. I believe it's gaining on us right along!" exclaimed Bluff.

"Look for a hollow tree!" cried Jerry.

"Humbug! Just because you once got in one during a storm you think a hollow tree can be used for nearly anything. Why, we'd be smothered in a jiffy, even if we didn't get burned to a crisp! Say something else!" shouted Bluff.

"What is it, Frank - you know?" demanded Will, who, in this time of need, somehow turned to the one whose cool head had many times managed to extricate them from some impending danger.

"We've just *got* to head another way, and try and get out of the path of the fire, if we can. Besides, the river lies to the left," he answered, as cheerily as he could.

"The river! Hurrah!" shrieked Will in sudden elation, for the very thought of water was a blessed relief when threatened by fire.

"We can duck under, and save our bacon!" cried Jerry.

"There you go, confessing to the swine again," declared Bluff.

But in spite of their light words the boys were by this time thoroughly alarmed. The appearance of the burning woods in their immediate rear was appalling, to say the least. High sprang the flames, and their crackling could now be plainly heard. Indeed, the sound began to assume the proportions of a continuous roar, such as a long freight train might make in passing over a trestle and down a grade.

Now that they were running almost sidewise to the advancing fire, it approached much faster than before.

"I felt a spark on my face, fellows!"

Frank was not at all surprised to hear Will say this, for he, too, had experienced the same thing not half a minute before. He had not mentioned the fact, for fear of alarming his chums still more.

"Keep on, fellows!" was all he said, for he needed every bit of breath he could muster.

Desperately they tried to increase their pace, but found it hard work with so many obstacles confronting them. Will tumbled more than any of the others, somehow or other. Perhaps it was because he was carrying his camera so carefully, and thinking more about it than his own person.

Finally Frank missed him entirely.

"Where's Will gone?" he demanded.

The others, turning, were horrified to find their chum missing.

"Keep right on, you fellows! Don't you dare stop, or follow me! I'll get Will! The river's close by!" he called out, and then turned around, retracing his steps directly toward the advancing fire.

Never had Will seemed so precious in the sight of the boy who thus placed his own life in jeopardy in order to save that of his chum. In imagination Frank pictured his agony of mind if he had to tell Violet that her twin brother had perished miserably in a forest fire, while he escaped.

"Will! Will!" he was shouting frantically, as loud as he could, and this was not anything to boast of, for the smoke choked him, and he could hardly keep from coughing almost constantly.

"Hi! Here I am! Lost like the babes in the woods!" sang out a voice.

Frank pounced on his friend, who, with smarting eyes, was fairly staggering about, hardly knowing which way he was trying to go, having become more or less rattled by the impending peril and the state of his own feelings.

"Run for all you're worth, Will!" he said, as he clutched the sleeve of the other almost fiercely, for they had little chance of eluding those hungry flames now.

Together they rushed along, Frank's eyes doing double duty, for Will seemed by this time half blind, and the one free hand was constantly rubbing his smarting orbs.

"A little further, and we're safe!" he kept calling in the ear of his nearly exhausted chum.

The heat was beginning to be terrific now. Blazing branches flew through the air, and set trees on fire all around them.

"It's like the fiery furnace!" Will said three times running, and Frank really began to fear his companion's mind was getting unsettled from the fright of their desperate condition.

Oh! if the river would only show up ahead! No doubt the others had, ere now, gained the glorious haven, and were settled up to their necks in the water, ready to defy the power of the opposing element. But it was an open question whether the halting pair could ever make the shelter of the friendly stream.

"Let me go, Frank! You can make it alone!" pleaded Will.

"Shut up! Keep on running! I tell you we're going to get there, and don't you think for a minute we ain't!" replied Frank furiously, as he pulled Will along.

CHAPTER XXII

THE WAR OF THE ELEMENTS

"This way, Frank! Turn a little to the left!"

"That's Jerry shouting! Do you hear him, Will? Keep up your heart! We're going to cheat the old fire yet!" cried Frank.

His companion seemed to pluck a little new spirit from the encouraging shout, and his lagging feet began to show more animation. In this way they hurried out of the already burning forest, and found themselves on the brink of the swift current of the valley stream.

"Jump in! The water's fine!" shouted Jerry, who, with Bluff, had submerged himself up to his shoulders.

"But my camera! I can't ruin it in the water!" shouted the obstinate Will, as he looked eagerly around for some place to conceal the object which he held in so much reverence.

"Under those rocks! We chucked our guns there!" called Bluff, pointing out the spot, in his eagerness to help matters along.

Will hastened to thrust the beloved camera into the cavity that lay beneath the rocks, and Frank, nothing loth, also pushed his rifle into the same place. Then it was ludicrous to see how quickly they made a plunge into the river.

Their immersion did not come a minute too soon. Frank knew that Will's garments were on fire in several places, and did not doubt but that his own must be in the same condition, for the sparks were raining all around them.

"This is all right," said the irrepressible Jerry, jumping up and down as he tried to hold out against the strong current.

"All I know is that we are in luck to have this blessed old river handy," said Frank, with more or less feeling in his voice, as he watched the fire flash from tree to tree in pursuing its course.

"Yes, it's a queer world. Only a few days ago it came near ending my life up at the cataract, and now it makes amends by saving it," remarked Jerry.

"The fire doesn't seem to jump across the river," observed Will.

"No; and I don't think it will, unless the wind changes quickly," said Frank.

"But it seems bound to get to our camp inside of an hour or two. What d'ye suppose they'll do with all the duffle?" inquired Bluff uneasily.

"I'm not worried about that. Mr. Mabie will scent trouble a long way off, and find a refuge among the rocks, if necessary; but I'm inclined to think the fire will never get to him," replied Frank.

"Do you believe the wind will shift, then, and blow back on us?" asked Will.

"I'm not a wind prophet. What I had in mind was that the fire would be put out before it got three miles from here."

"Put out! Do you mean to say they've a fire department up here?" demanded Will.

"Why, certainly; but it doesn't cost them a cent to maintain it. Somebody just pulls the string, and the water comes down," laughed Jerry.

"Oh! I see now what you mean! It's going to rain!"

"Hear! hear. He's tumbled to it at last! Sometimes it seems to me that we'll just have to get out a special dictionary for Will, so he can find the answers to conundrums without waste of time or energy," declared Bluff.

"That's the penalty every genius has to pay," remarked Will composedly.

Every now and then the boys were compelled to duck their heads beneath the surface of the river, for the heat became unbearable. When the worst of the fire had gone by on the wings of the furious wind, things began to change a bit for the better.

"Say! don't you think we might be getting out of here now?" demanded Will, whose teeth, strange to say, were rattling together with the chill of the mountain stream even while the air was still heated around them.

"I suppose it will be safe, and we can stand the heat if it will assist to dry our clothes. Though for that matter, fellows, it's ten to one we will be soaked through and through again before we get to camp."

"This is mighty unhealthy, I think. Such rapid changes always encourage dangerous ailments," remarked Will, whose father, now dead, had been a physician.

"All the same, I know several fellows who were very much pleased to make a sudden change a little while back," asserted Jerry.

They crawled out on the bank. Will, of course, made straight for the rocky niche toward which he had cast many an anxious look while standing in the river.

"Good! Everything is all right, boys! Not a bit of damage done, that I can see!" he called out.

They kept close to the river in making their way along. Perhaps the main idea in this was to have a handy refuge in case a sudden need arose.

"There she comes!" remarked Bluff, in less than ten minutes.

"What? Where?" asked Will, staring around.

A deep bellow of near-by thunder answered him. Then the rain began to fall in torrents. Will always carried a piece of waterproof cloth, to be used for wrapping around his precious camera on occasions when it was threatened with rain. This he brought into use, and at the same time tried to keep the little black box sheltered as much as possible under his coat.

From one extreme they had jumped to the other. First it was a superabundance of fire, and now water began to trouble them.

"I'm soaked through again," announced Jerry dolefully, as he allowed the wind to carry him along through the blackened timber.

"And I just bet that old fire has been squashed out before this," spluttered Bluff. "Don't you say so, Frank?"

"If it hasn't, it soon will be. Did you ever see it come down harder?"

"Must be trying to make up for the drouth of the last two months. Mr. Mabie said that when it did come we'd likely get a drencher. We're getting it, all right," declared Jerry.

For another half hour they kept on, though the walking was

very hard.

"A fine-looking crowd we are," declared Frank, as he surveyed his blackened leggings and sodden coat.

"But it seems to me things don't look quite so bad around here," observed Will.

"Well, they don't, for a fact. Frank, we've reached the fire limit, I do believe!" cried Bluff.

Everybody was glad to know it, for many reasons. The walking would be better, they could by degrees wash off the black stains that had been covering their clothes, and last, but far from least, the camp would be safe.

"I'll never forget this day's experience, that's sure," Jerry was saying, half an hour later, as, they still plodded on, with some miles still ahead of them that must be gone over before they reached camp.

"And every time I look at the picture of the fire it'll bob up before me and make me shudder," remarked Will.

"Talk to me about that, will you! Do you mean to say you had the nerve to stop and snap off some views of that hot old fire while the rest of us were shinning it as fast as we could?" demanded Jerry.

"Why, of course I did! What do you take me for? Who else would have preserved that exciting episode for future generations to enjoy, if I hadn't? That's what I'm here for," replied Will in surprise.

"And I suppose that was what made you so late Frank had to go back and hunt you up, eh?"

"I suppose it was, Bluff; but don't you scold now. I guess you'll enjoy those views as much as any one. There's only one thing I regret, fellows."

"And I can guess what that is. You wish you had taken the rest of us up to our chins in the drink," remarked Frank, whereat Will nodded eagerly, crying out:

"Oh! it would have been a great sight! Think how many times it might chase the blues away when some of us felt downcast! I wish, now, I had asked you to go back and give me the chance."

"Tell me about that, will you! Was there ever such an indefatigable - hey, Bluff! Is that the word I want? - artist as our meek little pard here? Sometimes he seems so timid, and then again he shows more nerve than the whole bunch put together. I thought I knew him to a dot, but I confess I'm puzzled," grunted Jerry.

"The rain has stopped, fellows," announced Frank a little later.

"But just look at the river! Must have been a cloudburst, as they call it out in the Rockies, Mr. Mabie says. It's just rising right before our eyes!"

"Then they'll have to change the camp, because by this time the water must be up to where the tents were pitched. Why, see there, Frank! Isn't that water over yonder, too, on the right of us?" asked Bluff, pointing through the woods.

"As sure as you live, and rushing madly on, too. We are between two rivers, it seems, with the water rising like a tidal wave. Perhaps we may have to take to a tree yet, fellows," announced Frank after a long look.

"H'm! These trees are sure handy to have around! We shin up one to avoid all sorts of dangers, it seems to me. And by the looks of that wall of water coming down on us just now, the sooner we climb, the better for us!" cried Jerry, suiting his actions to his words, and seizing the lower limb of a friendly oak, into which he clambered hastily, followed by his three chums, just as a five-foot wave swept under them, for all the world resembling a "curler" rolling in from the ocean and up the beach.

CHAPTER XXIII

THE STAMPEDE

"What d'ye call this, anyway?" exclaimed Bluff, panting with his exertions.

"I'd say it was crowding the mourners, for these things to chase each other so fast, and the elements to make playthings out of four confiding chums," said Frank.

"Tell me about that, will you! First a scorching, then put to soak, after which comes another hot experience, and now treed by a flood! Upon my word, things are happening a little too rapid even for me," put in Jerry.

"There!" remarked Will, with a satisfied chuckle. "I think you three fellows will make a splendid showing, perched along that limb like a lot of crows, and the water rolling along below."

"Talk to me about the industrious photographer! If that chap hasn't taken our pictures in this ridiculous attitude! Why, they'll believe we've gone back to the old days, when our ancestors used to live in trees."

"Speak for yourself, Jerry. I refuse to admit that I am descended from a monkey," declared Bluff indignantly.

"How long do you suppose we may have to hang out here?" asked Will.

"Oh, a day or so, I suppose," replied Jerry, keeping a straight face.

"A day or so! Listen to him say that without a show of feeling! Why, long before that time elapsed I'd grow so weak from fatigue that I'd have to be strapped to my limb to keep from falling into the treacherous water," stammered Will.

"And what of me?" burst out Bluff. "I'd waste away to a mere shadow from hunger. Sooner than submit to that, I'd try swimming ashore."

"Do you think the water will get any higher? Could it possibly overwhelm us in this tree? We could climb up twenty feet if necessary."

"Well, I hardly think that emergency is going to arise, Will; not at this time, at least. To tell the truth, the water is already receding," announced Frank, taking pity on Jerry's victims, both of whom looked worried.

"Oh! do you really think so?" cried Will. "Then Jerry is only up to some of his old foolishness. Yes, I can see that it does not quite come up to the wet mark on the trunk of the tree. Then perhaps we won't have to stay up here all night."

"Well, I guess not. I expect that in less than twenty minutes we'll be once more afoot, and on our way to camp. This must have been a genuine cloudburst, and they tell me those sort of things, while severe at the time, are quickly over."

"Bully for you, Frank! You always look on the bright side of things, while Jerry tries to dash a fellow's spirits. Things have come out pretty well, after all. We've had some strange experiences, come through them all in decent shape, and to cap the whole thing I've captured some dandy views. I can hardly wait to develop them."

"Go ahead, then. Plenty of water at hand for washing off the hypo," suggested Jerry wickedly.

By the time the twenty minutes had expired the water had subsided so far that the imprisoned chums were able to lower themselves from the tree and once more resume their journey.

Of course, they were an uncomfortable lot, being soaked to the skin, and, as Will declared, looking like a lot of hoboes. Brisk exertion kept them from feeling cold, however; but they were one and all delighted to set eyes on the familiar tents of the home camp.

Their welcome was a warm one, for Mr. Mabie had been more or less worried concerning them, owing to the forest fire and the fierce cloudburst.

"We hoped you were safe, and tried to believe it, boys; but at the same time, even a veteran hunter in these parts might have been caught napping, and I tell you we're mighty glad to see you back safe and sound. Now, tell us how it happened," was Mr. Mabie's greeting as he squeezed a hand of each.

"If you mean the fire, sir, we know nothing about it. We have not struck a match since leaving here, and only Bluff shot once. The fire came from an entirely different quarter, I assure you," said Frank.

"I never doubted that, my lad. I've seen enough of you boys to know that after all I've said none of you would be careless enough to endanger things. But perhaps, after all, the fire was more of a blessing than otherwise, for it probably helped to hurry that rainstorm along, and that has saved our pastures."

Of course, the boys were for getting into dry clothes at once. The fire was heaped high with fresh fuel, so that a delightful warmth would be diffused around the immediate vicinity, after which there was a general change of garments.

"I feel better than I thought I would after all that rumpus," admitted Bluff, as he capered about, trying to keep his muscles from getting stiff.

"We'll look back to this day as one of the strangest in all our experience," remarked Frank, hanging his wet garments where the sun would fall upon them, for the clouds had passed away, leaving a clear sky overhead.

"How much longer do we stay here?" asked Will, who had been doing some figuring. "Because my films are getting low. I have three rolls still at the ranch house, and when they're exhausted my business is done."

"Sorry to tell you, lads, that I had word from the house while you were gone, and it's absolutely necessary for me to start back in the morning. Now, if you would like to remain a little longer in camp, why, Reddy and Billy will keep you company. Don't give up unless you're satisfied with what fun you've had," said the stockman just then.

The boys looked at each other.

"I think we've seen enough of this life, and that there are dozens of things about the ranch we ought to know more about. So I vote that we return with Mr. Mabie," was Frank's suggestion.

"Count me in that," echoed Jerry.

"And I'm just wild to print a few of the remarkable pictures I've made up here, which I can't do until we get back to the house; so I'm only too willing to say yes to the proposition," put in Will.

"And I'm just as happy one place as the other, so long as the cook doesn't strike, or put us on short rations," added Bluff.

In this spirit of humor it was therefore decided that on the following morning they would break camp and return to the ranch.

"I feel that I'm cheating you out of some of your expected fun, boys," apologized the stockman that evening, as they were packing some of their stuff, so as to lighten the labor in the morning.

"Why, I don't know what else we could do here. Seems to me we've about exhausted the list of excitements. We've shot elk, grizzlies, a panther, a wolf, met up with Indians, been chased by a forest fire, soaked in the river and treed by a cloudburst. There could hardly be anything more, sir," laughed Frank.

"Well, I admit that you have made hay while the sun shone; and such a pushing lot of boys always will get all the fun there is going. It's been the happiest event of my last ten years of life to have you with me, and when you see my old side partner of long ago just tell him that I'll never get over being thankful to him for having sent you up here to break the dreadful monotony of existence on a stock ranch."

They passed a delightful evening. The boys sang many of their school songs, and Bluff was induced to give a recitation, which called forth vociferous applause from the cowboy audience.

"I can see very plainly that you are going to make a worthy successor to that lawyer father of yours, Bluff," declared Mr. Mabie as he clapped his hands.

"And I expect to live to see him on the Supreme Bench yet," said Jerry seriously.

In the morning preparations for their departure were soon completed. The tents, and all material connected with the camp, went in the wagon, while the boys, together with Mr. Mabie and Reddy, rode horseback. It was an invigorating gallop back to the ranch house, and on the way the chums indulged in a number of little races. But Will would not allow himself to enter as he was afraid that something might happen to his precious camera, which he carried by a strap over his shoulder.

Once back in their old quarters, for several days the boys took life easy, each being busily engaged in some favorite pursuit. Will developed all his films, and made copious prints of the same, which kept him in a feverish state of mind. When one turned out especially fine he was in the seventh heaven of delight; and if he met with disappointment, which was seldom the case, his laments were dismal indeed.

Thus a week more passed, and the boys were beginning to think of turning their faces toward the East again. They would leave the ranch with many regrets, for Mr. Mabie had certainly quite won their youthful hearts by his genial ways.

Frank was the last one to meet with an adventure on this occasion, which was fated to be written down in his logbook as worthy of remembrance.

He had been out riding, and his horse, stepping into a gopher hole, threw him. Frank was not seriously hurt, but the horse went lame, so that he could not be ridden. As this happened miles away from the house, and night was coming on, with a storm threatening, Frank knew he was in for an experience; but even then he did not dream of all that was down on the bills for that special occasion.

Through the darkness he went, leading his limping horse. Then the storm broke, and the crash of thunder, as well as the vivid lightning, was something such as he could not remember ever meeting before.

He was just thinking that the pony had recovered enough to enable him to mount and make his way slowly along, as the ranch house was not more than a mile off, when something came to his ears that arrested his attention. For half a minute he wondered what it might be, sounding like increasing thunder. Then the appalling truth flashed upon him. There

was a stampede of cattle, and he seemed to be directly in the way of the madly galloping herd!

CHAPTER XXIV

A MYSTERY SOLVED

Frank, after that one spasm of alarm, gritted his teeth, and thought fast. He had heard the rancher, as well as the cowboys, speak of the terrors of the stampede, when the cattle were in a frenzy, through fear, and utterly beyond all management.

He knew that frequently experienced cowmen, caught in the rush of a thousand lumbering steers, had been ground to death under countless hoofs. It was so in the old days, when bison dotted the plains of the great West.

Mounted on a good horse, one might hope to ride clear of the advancing avalanche of hoofs and horns. But his steed was lame, and hardly able to limp along. The situation was one calculated to arouse a boy as he had never been awakened before in all his life.

Frank jumped upon the back of his horse. He knew instantly that his one hope must lie in getting clear of the immense herd; and that this could only be done by either riding faster than they were going down the wide valley, or in making for the nearest hillside, where trees would offer him a refuge.

He chose the latter. Flight in a straightaway course was utterly out of the question with a cripple between his knees.

"Get up, Hector! Do your prettiest now!" he called to his horse.

The poor beast was trying his hardest to run well, but making only a pretense, after all, since that lame leg kept him from speedy progress. Doubtless Hector, being a cow pony, knew full well the nature of the peril that menaced them, and if it lay in his power he would bear his young master to a point of safety.

Frank's heart seemed to be in his throat as he leaned forward and listened to the rapidly approaching roar of hundreds upon hundreds of hoofs, mingled with the horrid clashing of horns. Added to this was the deep-toned thunder and the dazzling flashes of lightning.

Once, when he looked to the left, he could see the moving mass that was sweeping horribly close. After that he resolutely kept his attention riveted in front, where the ridge loomed up against the darkened heavens.

Everything depended upon how far he was from the nearest trees. Seconds counted with Frank just then. The lightning flashed every quarter of a minute, and yet it seemed to him that they were ages apart.

With his heart in his throat, as it seemed, he stared ahead, and waited for the next flash to show him the worst. Unless the trees were close by, his case seemed hopeless, for the main herd appeared to have pushed over to this side of the valley, unfortunately, showing that he had picked the wrong course when he started.

Hector stumbled more than once, and Frank feared he would be thrown. He even wondered whether it would not be better for him to throw himself to the ground while he had the chance, and trust to his own legs to carry him to safety.

Then came the eagerly anticipated flash. Hope sprang anew in his breast, for he had discovered the trees close at hand. One more gallant effort on the part of the crippled pony, and they managed to pass behind the outposts of the timber, just as the beginning of the terrible rushing stampede swept by.

There Frank sat upon his pony, breathing hard, and patting the poor animal reassuringly. He could hear the loud cries of the cowboys and Mr. Mabie as they circled about the terrified cattle, trying by every means possible to influence them to mill; but in that gloom it was impossible to carry out the usual tactics, and by degrees the sounds died away far down the valley.

Frank walked with his lame pony to the ranch house. Here he found his chums in a fright because of his absence. They were afraid he had been caught in the mad stampede and ground under the hoofs of the steers.

Mr. Mabie did not show up until long after midnight. The storm had passed away, and the sky cleared by that time. The boys were sitting up, waiting, none of them thinking of seeking his bed.

"Hello, Frank, my lad! I'm mighty glad to find you here, safe and sound. I saw your pony at the stable, and that you had bound up his leg, showing a sprain. But I was afraid that something more serious had been the matter. You don't know how relieved I was to see your horse; and Reddy, too. The poor fellow has been in a sweat with fear ever since the stampede broke out," was the hearty way the rancher greeted Frank as he came bustling in.

"Oh, I was right in the line of the rush, but by clever work on the part of my pony managed to reach the trees before they caught me. But what's the report about the cattle, sir?" asked Frank eagerly.

"The boys have halted them about ten miles from here. Thanks to the storm stopping, and the animals getting leg weary, we managed to head them off. Little damage done, except to our feelings. These things happen once in a while, and are really unavoidable. Steers in a panic are crazy; but then I suppose the same would apply to human beings, if all accounts are true that I read about theater fires and such things."

He asked many questions concerning Frank's adventure.

"You just happened to choose the wrong side, lad. Had you headed the other way you would have had little trouble. The storm came from that quarter, and a cowboy must have known that cattle always run *away* from the lightning and rain. But fortunately you made the timber, and; as the subject is unpleasant, we'll drop it for the present. Now get off to bed, the lot of you. In the morning, if you want, I'll take you down with me, and show you how we drive a big herd."

"I've got my last roll of films in the camera, and that would make a mighty fine set of pictures to finish up with; but, oh! what wouldn't I give if I could have caught Frank, here, riding for life on that crippled pony, and the stampede sweeping down on him!" said Will enthusiastically.

"Talk to me about your cold-blooded savages! Does anything equal a crank with a camera, bent on snapping off everything that happens?" muttered Jerry, shaking his head in real or assumed disgust.

"That is the fate of every genius, to be misunderstood and misrepresented when ready to sacrifice comfort and everything to his art. But I am not the only one who is a crank. I have known fellows so proud of their lungs, that night after night they insisted on filling the air mattresses of the party just to prove which could blow the harder; while the other two members of the party sat by and laughed."

Frank chuckled at hearing this, and both Bluff and Jerry looked daggers, for the shot hit home with them.

In the morning the boys did accompany the rancher down the valley. Frank showed them his course on the previous night, and they followed his line of travel until the trees were reached. Trail there was none, for hundreds of cloven hoofs had pounded the soil about that spot, showing how narrow had been his escape.

The cowboys were found to have the big herd well in hand. It was even then on the way back to its former feeding ground. Some of the steers showed the effects of the mad rush, in various cuts from the horns of their fellows; and several had tripped and gone down to death in the panic, the herd trampling them into an unrecognizable mass.

Of course, Will satisfied his longing, and secured what pictures he wanted.

"I'm happy in having carried out my plans. Won't the home folks stare when they see the panorama of views I've gathered!" he said jubilantly.

"I should think they would," remarked Jerry, shrugging his shoulders, "for you certainly have a collection of freak pictures, some of which would take the prize."

"But all of this lot are genuine. Nobody had to prance around a tree with a dead yellow dog on his feet, pretending to chase after him," asserted Will.

"Whose doing was that, eh? Tell me that! Didn't you just plead with me to make a fool of myself, and to save you pain I consented. I suppose I'll never hear the end of that fool joke," growled Jerry.

"Oh, yes, you will. It's all in the family. Others don't know the dog was dead when he had his picture taken. They all say he looks as though about to snap a piece out of your leg. Now, I think we've just had a glorious time of it up here, with nothing to mar our pleasure," remarked Frank, the peacemaker.

"Except that miserable job of mine in leaving my knife home," sighed Bluff.

"Talk to me about that, will you! He hasn't forgotten it yet!" exclaimed Jerry.

"I never can. Hello! Here comes Reddy with a bag of mail, the last we'll get, I suppose, before we go home. A letter for me? Now just keep your eyes to yourselves, fellows. I admit it's from Nellie, but no doubt the dear girl is anxious about her brother Frank, and wants information from a thoroughly reliable quarter."

Bluff sought out a lonesome corner of the big piazza in front of the ranch house, and presently all hands were absorbed in their letters. Suddenly the others heard Bluff utter an exclamation, and looked up just in time to see him sprint into the building.

"What d'ye suppose ails the fellow?" asked Will.

"Give it up. He seemed to have a broad grin on his face, as though Nellie must have written something especially sweet. But here he comes out again, dancing like a wild Indian. What's he waving above his head, fellows?" said Frank.

"It's his lost hunting-knife, as sure as you live!" echoed Will.

"Just to think of it, boys! The beauty was in my clothes bag all the time, and I didn't know it! Nellie did it. She mentions the fact in this letter, and says she was so afraid I'd hurt myself with that knife, by accident, that she rolled it up in this new flannel shirt, which I've never thought to put on as yet, and thrust it down at the bottom of my clothes bag. I never thought to pull it out; and now that the big-game hunt is over I get my trusty blade."

"Tell me about that, will you! And you thought I was to blame," remarked Jerry.

"For which I beg your pardon. After all, perhaps no harm was done, and since Nellie only did it from the best of motives, why, I would be foolish to be angry."

"Sensible for once," observed Frank, winking at the others.

"And so we will leave the ranch without the slightest cloud on the horizon. Fellows, all I can say is we're a lucky lot of boys," observed Will positively.

CHAPTER XXV

HOME AGAIN - CONCLUSION

Saying good-by was harder than the boys had anticipated. They had really enjoyed themselves so immensely up there at the ranch in the wilderness that the thought of never seeing it more brought gloom upon their spirits.

Of course, the fact that they were heading toward home, and the dear ones awaiting their coming, made their sorrow lighter.

They had sent their trunk away on the previous evening, so that it would be at the far distant station awaiting their coming. On horseback, then, they were to cover the route that on their arrival they had done on a buckboard.

Mr. Mabie, Reddy and Billy accompanied them, the stockman and Billy to bring back the mounts after the train had borne their young friends away. Reddy, of course, expected to accompany the boys East, to at least visit his family. He could not promise to remain at home, for the magic of the magnificent country of the Northwest called loudly to him; but he was taking home his savings, and meant to make his parents happy.

"I'll never forget all the good times you've given us, Mr. Mabie," said Frank, as he squeezed the hand of their good friend when the whistle of the approaching train was heard as it came booming out of the cut, a mile away.

"My dear boy, on my part I can never thank you and your jolly chums half enough for the delightful time you've given me. It will seem dreary here after you're gone. I haven't been so happy for years," was the reply of the stockman, as he beamed upon the cluster of bright faces around him.

"But you know you promised to make us a visit when we're home from college next Christmas. Don't forget that, sir!" declared Will.

"I certainly will not, if I'm alive. And Will, one of the inducements for such a long journey is the expectation of seeing that remarkable book of interesting views, containing reminders of so many of the exploits of the Outdoor Club. I'm sure that alone would repay me for the trip," laughed the other.

"You won't forget about shipping those skins and things, sir? We want them for reminders of the happiest trip this club ever took. Every time we look at those rugs we'll think of you and your Big M ranch," remarked Bluff.

"They'll go in a few days, boys, just as soon as the skins are in proper shape for transportation, depend on it. And I'll let you know when Pierre is placed under arrest, and the exiled chief, Running Elk, goes back to his people with all honor."

The last they saw of Mr. Mabie and Billy, they were waving their big hats vigorously on the little station platform. Then a curve of the road shut them out, and the four chums settled back in their seats to talk over the thousand and one matters that claimed their attention.

It is not in youth to grieve for long. They felt bad at leaving the scene of these recent happy events; but presently, in anticipation of the reunion with loved ones at home, this was temporarily forgotten.

Will bemoaned the fact that he had not one single film left.

"And there are so many things I'd like to take on the way home," he sighed, "and which I let slip on the way up."

"Yes," remarked Jerry laughingly, "it's wonderful what game you see when you haven't a gun. But what's the matter with you trying to get a roll at the first town? Perhaps we may stop long enough, and they may have photographic supplies at the station."

"Thank you for the suggestion, Jerry. It was a bright thought - for you; but I mean to take advantage of it, and make inquiries."

Jerry gave him a queer look. Will was a fellow he could not fully understand. He seemed to be made up of contradictions, sometimes simple, and again shrewd; now as timid as a girl, and under certain conditions showing the bravery of a lion. Jerry knew Bluff as he did his own nature, and could dispute with him with energy, but in the case of Will he was always glad to drop the subject before he found he had burned his fingers.

Nothing of moment happened on the journey, at least nothing worthy of mention. Will did manage to secure a roll of films at the first town. A messenger came to the car with it, and Frank always supposed from that that his eccentric companion must have wired ahead for supplies. When Will wanted anything he meant to get it, if there was any possible way of so doing.

In due time they arrived at the station in Centerville, where a host of relatives and friends awaited their coming. There was a roar of many voices as the four chums appeared in view, and our boys quickly found themselves being hugged and kissed in a most indiscriminate fashion.

If some of the girls, in the confusion, kissed the brothers of their friends, as well as their own, that was not to be wondered at, and everybody seemed as happy as could be, despite these natural blunders.

Finally they managed to push outside the station.

"Where's Hank Brady?" called Frank aloud.

"Here!" said that worthy, stepping forward from the motor-car, and holding out his hand eagerly to the friend who had been so instrumental in assisting him to get his slipping feet on steady ground.

"Hello, Hank! Here's your brother Teddy!"

In this abrupt fashion did he bring the two face to face. Hank turned white, and stared hard at the bronzed young cowboy for a moment; then he caught hold of him, and the long separated; brothers were in each other's arms.

"Sure, the old folks will be happy this night, Ted, to see you again! I never hoped they'd find you when I asked Mr. Frank to keep on the lookout," was what Hank was saying, as he turned a moist eye in the direction of the boy who had done so much to bring happiness to his home.

Bluff and Nellie were seen talking earnestly close by. Probably he was telling her about the surprise she gave him in that last letter when revealing what she had done with his wonderful hunting-knife.

Now that they were home again, with vacation nearing an end, the boys would not have so much time to indulge in their pastimes on the lake, so that they were keen to make hay while the sun shone. Consequently, they fairly haunted the lake, and the canoes were in use every day from that time on. Nor were they alone in this love of the open, for many an evening each canoe had its complement of fair ones, whose sweet voices blended with those of the four outdoor chums as they paddled in the moonlight over the rippling water.

College was ahead of them, but as they expected to keep together still, the Outdoor Club was not to be disbanded by any means. Often in future days they expected to once more sit around a campfire in company, enjoying the delights of an outing, and recalling many of the wonderful experiences that came their way in days that were past.

And there, written down in Frank's diary, or logbook, were the accounts of their first camp above the loggers' settlement, at the head of the lake; the one on Wildcat Island; then the third, among the Sunset Mountains, when they solved the mystery of Oak Ridge's ghost; and also their wonderful cruise down a Florida river and along the border of the great Mexican Gulf; while this journey to the cattle ranch of Mr. Mabie, in the wilderness of the Northwest, would complete the list.

How many times, as they read of these exploits, and surveyed the splendid pictures Will had secured during their various campaigns, would the scenes of the happy past come before their mental vision! They could hardly expect to equal these glorious days in the times to come, but no one who knew their love for the open would dare predict that the Outdoor Club would cease to exist with the going to college of its four members.

Perchance they may yet have other camps in strange places, and perhaps it may be our pleasant duty to chronicle the happenings of the four chums when again they erect their tents, or it may be, paddle their canoes on other waters.

Wherever they go, and in whatever line of business they may find their life work, it can be taken for granted that the lessons learned when living this life of self-reliance in the open must always prove of the greatest value to The Outdoor Chums.

George Eliot
George Gissing
George MacDonald
George Meredith
George Orwell
George Sylvester Viereck
George Tucker
George W. Cable
George Wharton James
Gertrude Atherton
Gordon Casserly
Grace E. King
Grace Gallatin
Grace Greenwood
Grant Allen
Guillermo A. Sherwell
Gulielma Zollinger
Gustav Flaubert
H. A. Cody
H. B. Irving
H.C. Bailey
H. G. Wells
H. H. Munro
H. Irving Hancock
H. Rider Haggard
H. W. C. Davis
Haldeman Julius
Hall Caine
Hamilton Wright Mabie
Hans Christian Andersen
Harold Avery
Harold McGrath
Harriet Beecher Stowe
Harry Castlemon
Harry Coghill
Harry Houidini
Hayden Carruth
Helent Hunt Jackson
Helen Nicolay
Hendrik Conscience
Hendy David Thoreau
Henri Barbusse
Henrik Ibsen
Henry Adams
Henry Ford
Henry Frost
Henry James
Henry Jones Ford
Henry Seton Merriman
Henry W Longfellow
Herbert A. Giles
Herbert Carter
Herbert N. Casson
Herman Hesse
Hildegard G. Frey
Homer
Honore De Balzac
Horace B. Day
Horace Walpole
Horatio Alger Jr.
Howard Pyle
Howard R. Garis
Hugh Lofting
Hugh Walpole
Humphry Ward
Ian Maclaren
Inez Haynes Gillmore
Irving Bacheller
Isabel Hornibrook
Israel Abrahams
Ivan Turgenev
J.G.Austin
J. Henri Fabre
J. M. Barrie
J. Macdonald Oxley
J. S. Fletcher
J. S. Knowles
J. Storer Clouston
Jack London
Jacob Abbott
James Allen
James Andrews
James Baldwin
James Branch Cabell
James DeMille
James Joyce
James Lane Allen
James Lane Allen
James Oliver Curwood
James Oppenheim
James Otis
James R. Driscoll
Jane Austen
Jane L. Stewart
Janet Aldridge
Jens Peter Jacobsen
Jerome K. Jerome
John Burroughs
John Cournos
John F. Kennedy
John Gay
John Glasworthy
John Habberton
John Joy Bell
John Kendrick Bangs
John Milton
John Philip Sousa
Jonas Lauritz Idemil Lie
Jonathan Swift
Joseph A. Altsheler
Joseph Carey
Joseph Conrad
Joseph E. Badger Jr
Joseph Hergesheimer
Joseph Jacobs
Jules Vernes
Julian Hawthrone
Julie A Lippmann
Justin Huntly McCarthy
Kakuzo Okakura
Kenneth Grahame
Kenneth McGaffey
Kate Langley Bosher
Kate Langley Bosher
Katherine Cecil Thurston
Katherine Stokes
L. A. Abbot
L. T. Meade
L. Frank Baum
Latta Griswold
Laura Dent Crane
Laura Lee Hope
Laurence Housman
Lawrence Beasley
Leo Tolstoy
Leonid Andreyev
Lewis Carroll
Lewis Sperry Chafer
Lilian Bell
Lloyd Osbourne
Louis Hughes
Louis Tracy
Louisa May Alcott
Lucy Fitch Perkins
Lucy Maud Montgomery
Luther Benson
Lydia Miller Middleton
Lyndon Orr
M. Corvus
M. H. Adams
Margaret E. Sangster
Margret Howth
Margaret Vandercook

Margret Penrose
Maria Edgeworth
Maria Thompson Daviess
Mariano Azuela
Marion Polk Angellotti
Mark Overton
Mark Twain
Mary Austin
Mary Catherine Crowley
Mary Cole
Mary Hastings Bradley
Mary Roberts Rinehart
Mary Rowlandson
M. Wollstonecraft Shelley
Maud Lindsay
Max Beerbohm
Myra Kelly
Nathaniel Hawthrone
Nicolo Machiavelli
O. F. Walton
Oscar Wilde
Owen Johnson
P.G. Wodehouse
Paul and Mabel Thorne
Paul G. Tomlinson
Paul Severing
Percy Brebner
Peter B. Kyne
Plato
R. Derby Holmes
R. L. Stevenson
R. S. Ball
Rabindranath Tagore
Rahul Alvares
Ralph Bonehill
Ralph Henry Barbour
Ralph Victor
Ralph Waldo Emmerson
Rene Descartes
Rex Beach
Rex E. Beach
Richard Harding Davis
Richard Jefferies
Richard Le Gallienne
Robert Barr
Robert Frost
Robert Gordon Anderson
Robert L. Drake
Robert Lansing
Robert Lynd
Robert Michael Ballantyne
Robert W. Chambers
Rosa Nouchette Carey
Rudyard Kipling
Samuel B. Allison
Samuel Hopkins Adams
Sarah Bernhardt
Sarah C. Hallowell
Selma Lagerlof
Sherwood Anderson
Sigmund Freud
Standish O'Grady
Stanley Weyman
Stella Benson
Stella M. Francis
Stephen Crane
Stewart Edward White
Stijn Streuvels
Swami Abhedananda
Swami Parmananda
T. S. Ackland
T. S. Arthur
The Princess Der Ling
Thomas A. Janvier
Thomas A Kempis
Thomas Anderton
Thomas Bailey Aldrich
Thomas Bulfinch
Thomas De Quincey
Thomas Dixon
Thomas H. Huxley
Thomas Hardy
Thomas More
Thornton W. Burgess
U. S. Grant
Valentine Williams
Various Authors
Vaughan Kester
Victor Appleton
Victoria Cross
Virginia Woolf
Wadsworth Camp
Walter Camp
Walter Scott
Washington Irving
Wilbur Lawton
Wilkie Collins
Willa Cather
Willard F. Baker
William Dean Howells
William le Queux
W. Makepeace Thackeray
William W. Walter
William Shakespeare
Winston Churchill
Yei Theodora Ozaki
Yogi Ramacharaka
Young E. Allison
Zane Grey

www.ingramcontent.com/pod-product-compliance
Lightning Source LLC
LaVergne TN
LVHW090608110826
845146LV00001B/302

* 9 7 8 1 4 2 1 8 2 5 0 0 7 *